THE DOG WAS ADOPTED TOO

Judy Glover Smith

PUBLISHED by PARABLES
Earthly Stories with a Heavenly Meaning

The Dog Was Adopted Too
Copyright © Judy Glover Smith
Published By Parables

All Rights Reserved. No part of this book may be reproduced or utilized in any form or by any means, electronic or mechanical, including photocopying, recording, or by any information storage and retrieval system, without permission in writing from the author.

Unless otherwise specified Scripture quotations are taken from the authorized version of the King James Bible.

First Edition May,, 2016

ISBN 978-0-9974392-4-3

Printed in the United States of America

Readers should be aware that Internet Web sites offered as citations and/or sources for further information may have been changed or disappeared between the time this was written and when it is read.

Illustration provided by www.unsplash.com

THE DOG WAS ADOPTED TOO
Judy Glover Smith

PUBLISHED by PARABLES
Earthly Stories with a Heavenly Meaning

Table of Contents

	Title Page	
	Table of Contents	
	Acknowledgements	1
	Word to Parents and Teachers	2
	Introduction	3
1	The Accident	5
2	Startled	10
3	The Sound	16
4	A fine Young Man	20
5	Wally!	24
6	The Emergency	29
7	It's Not Your Fault	36
8	An Out of Season Fire	42
9	No Ordinary Boat Ride	52
10	The Broken Toy	61
11	He's the One	69
12	The Tickets	76
13	Favorite Story	81
14	Strike	87
15	The Short Hallway	92
16	The Mud Story	96
17	A Looming Figure	104
18	This is Really Great!	112
19	New Beginnings	117
20	The Contest	126
21	Praise in the Park	131
	Credits	137

THE DOG WAS ADOPTED TOO

ACKNOWLEDGMENTS

I wish to thank God for allowing me to write this book. May it glorify His Holy name.

Many thanks to my friends who proof read this book:

My husband, Lester Smith,
who has read this book more times than I can remember.
Martha Allen
Edna Frierson
Pam Holt
Claudia Lane
Frances McIntire
Dr. Tobey Pitman
Claudine Reed
Donna Rosche
Peggy H. Seeley
Darnell Songy
Aurora Williams

I also wish to thank those who have constantly encouraged and prayed for me:

My family
Ladies Bible Study
First Baptist Church of Pearl River
The Armor of God Prayer Group

Judy Glover Smith

A Word To Parents and Teachers

The Dog Was Adopted, Too is full of smiles, laughter, surprise, suspense, and emotion. Although the loss of or separation from loved ones is part of the story line, no person or animal dies within the time line of this book. This may be a good point to share with younger, more sensitive or anxious readers.

The Dog Was Adopted, Too was written with the intention of teaching how to overcome problems through prayer, family, friendship, and God's intervention.

The age range of The Dog Was Adopted, Too readers is from the third to ninth grades, however, both younger and older readers have expressed enjoyment from reading the book or having it read to them. Group reading, whether at home or at school, is a good time to discuss salvation and answer any questions that may be asked. It will also give the leader an opportunity to discuss character development without causing anyone to feel as though he or she is being singled out.

It is my desire that the older or more independent readers will sit back and enjoy the pages themselves. Individual reading will give the opportunity to discover Biblical truths for themselves.

I pray that the reader may learn what "Abba, Father" means and how to accept His adoption.

Romans 8:14-15
"For as many as are led by the Spirit of God, they are the sons of God.
 For ye have not received the spirit of bondage again to fear; but ye have received the Spirit of adoption, whereby we cry, Abba, Father."

Introduction
The Dog Was Adopted Too

Alex Foster lives with his parents, Roger and Rebecca, and his sister Leora. The Fosters are a loving family; full of respect, with lots of hugs and friendly interaction. Their family has always regularly attended church.

Alex is blessed by life-long friends at school and at church. Most afternoons you can find Alex hanging out with his four closest friends: Michael, Derick, and Joshua Davis and Kevin Oliver. Their favorite place to meet is at the local park gazebo. Through the years, the gazebo has served as a mighty frontier fortress; a great sailing vessel with cannons; a space craft chasing aliens throughout the cosmos; a western ranch for horses or cattle; a treacherous mountain cabin complete with bears; or a vast array of any other exciting imaginary posts.

Currently, the goal of each boy is to be the weekly contest winner in the boy's Sunday school class. The students who choose to compete are required to read the assigned Bible story during the week. The following Sunday, each boy is expected to bring a list of interesting facts to win the prize. To qualify, the boys must be on time for class with their entries. If a boy is late, he is disqualified for that week.

Mr. Walker, the boys Sunday school teacher, owns the local bowling alley and awards each week's winner with two bowling passes; one for the winner and another for his guest. At times, all the boys are competitive and usually a different boy wins each week.

Alex is a good boy, but he has one major problem. He is usually self-centered. If he loses the Sunday school contest too often, he becomes cranky. To be perfectly honest, all of the boys have this same personality trait.

Theodore Moore, the new boy in town, had a major tragedy in his life which caused him to be adopted by his Uncle Samuel and Aunt Betty Bennett. He attends the same school and church that Alex and his friends attend.

Theodore desperately needs friends, however, the tragedy has caused him to become withdrawn and he doesn't know how to reach out to anyone. When he first joined the Sunday school class, he saw how much fun the contests were. The boys always cheered for the winners and talked about how much fun they had bowling. This activity looked like just the thing that Theodore wanted, so he began competing. He won every week, but unfortunately, his winning was not well received by the class. No one applauded because they thought he was just butting in, and they rejected him. This resulted in Theodore isolating himself by sitting alone in the back of the class. Isolation caused the other boys to ignore him, leading him to spiral deeper into depression.

God begins using a friendly neighborhood dog named Wally to change the hearts of the boys. God touches Alex and his friends which causes them to become aware of the needs of Theodore. God also brings the awareness of Jesus to Theodore's broken heart.

We begin the story at the point where God begins His work. Alex is headed toward his Sunday school class with his contest entry in hand. He remembers that donuts are served in the guest greeting room and takes a detour. Turn to chapter one to become part of Alex's week long journey of challenges and discoveries.

CHAPTER ONE
SUNDAY MORNING
THE ACCIDENT

"I'm late," Alex Foster scolded himself as he squeezed past the people in the Greeting Room and hurried outside. "No donuts. What a waste of time." Alex trotted around the corner of the building and looked at his watch.

"Two minutes!" he shrieked. "I'm going to miss the contest." His panic sent him into a dead-run.

It was a bright, sunlit morning with a sky full of fluffy clouds. Normally, he would have searched for animal shapes among the clouds, but today he didn't even look up as he ran.

Setting his sights on the opened educational building door, he flew from the bright daylight into the seemingly dark Sunday school building. As he skidded around the first corner, he accelerated until he saw the silhouettes of four giggling girls standing in a small circle. He locked his feet, trying to stop, but his momentum made his shoes slide uncontrollably on the shiny, freshly waxed floor. He felt like a bowling ball speeding down an alley. Unable to avoid the girls, he crossed his arms over his eyes as he slid into them. The crash seemed to shake the building.

Stumbling to a stop, he grabbed a chair to avoid falling. He said to himself, "Well, that had to be a bowling strike."

He waited for his eyes to adjust to the inside light, then turned slowly to survey his path of destruction. He saw two girls getting up, another leaning against the wall, and a fourth sprawled out on the floor. There were Bibles and Sunday school materials scattered everywhere.

He walked toward the girls, recognizing them as he neared. Billie and Ariel threw icy stares at him as they straightened their hair and clothes. "Oh, no!" he thought, "Only two of the cutest girls in town." He felt doomed as he realized that it was Susan, the pastor's daughter, who was leaning against the wall glaring at him.

He grimaced as he looked down at the swaying girl who was still sitting on the floor. Previous worries popped like balloons. He stepped quickly forward, silently begging, "Please be okay! Please be okay!"

He reached out to her and meekly asked, "Are you alright, Mom?"

"What happened?" she asked as she pushed her hair back and reached for Alex's hand. He took his mom's hand and helped her up as he looked around at the angry faces.

He decided to answer first. "I'm sorry. I couldn't see. It was dark and I didn't mean to bump into you."

Ariel shouted, "Bump?" as she gathered her books from the floor.

Alex heard laughter behind him and looked around. From classroom doors, he saw smiling faces and heard voices asking, "What was that?"

"Is everyone okay?"

"Did you see that?"

But the statement that turned his embarrassment into despair was, "Uh-oh! Look!" Alex turned slowly and saw his dad picking up the scattered articles.

With a low voice, Dad glanced up and said, "We'll discuss this when we get home. Go to class."

Alex, without saying a word, obediently crossed the hall to Mr. Walker's class. He gave his crumpled paper to his teacher, who said, "What was all that noise?"

Alex could hear quiet snickering as he passed his friends on his way to his usual spot at the table.

"Nice going, Hulk," whispered Michael.

"Way to go," said Joshua.

Quietly, Kevin stated, "That's not how you're supposed to make girls fall for you."

Derick raised his hand for a high-five, which Alex ignored.

Mr. Walker said, "Last week I assigned 'The Young Daniel' which is found in the book of Daniel chapter one. From these scriptures, you were to find interesting details about this important Bible character. Mr. Jenkins will check your answers. I'll let you know at the end of the class who receives the two bowling passes for winning today's contest. Do you have any questions?"

He looked around and not receiving an answer, said, "Today's lesson shows that God allowed Daniel to have both good and bad experiences. This taught him that he could trust God during good or bad times. This lesson teaches that you can trust God everyday of your life."

Alex opened his book and wondered how this bad time could teach him anything.

Mr. Walker continued, "Daniel, as a child, had lived with his family in Jerusalem. The Babylonians kidnapped Daniel and his friends, and trained them to be servants in the king's palace. When the boys were fed the king's rich foods, Daniel asked if he and his friends could be fed the foods approved by God. The guard agreed, and after ten days noticed that Daniel and his friends were healthier than the other boys. After three years of training, King Nebuchadnezzar was impressed by Daniel and his friends and placed them on his staff of advisors. God continued to use and bless Daniel throughout his life."

Alex tried to listen, but he couldn't get the contest or his dad's promised lecture out of his thoughts. He sighed to himself, "What a day. Well, when I win, everything will be different." He looked at Theodore and thought proudly, "He won't win today. This lesson was tough." The night before he had watched one of his mom's movies about Daniel and was sure he would win. He turned his back to Theodore and thought smugly, "The best the new kid can do is to tie with me."

Alex sat up straight when Mr. Walker put his Bible down. Mr. Jenkins, his assistant, gave him the score sheet, which he silently read.

Mr. Walker looked up and said, "Don't forget about the special church service in the park next week. It is called 'Praise in the Park'. Be ready to share what God has done in your life. Now, let's get back to the contest. I found fourteen items. Five of you competed today, and as a group, you came up with ten items.

"Ten!" Alex grumbled under his breath, "I wonder who the winner is. I hope it's not..."

"Theodore is today's winner, again!" Mr. Walker proudly announced.

Alex slumped as he thought, "Well, his parents probably found the answers for him."

The disappointed class watched silently as, once again, Theodore rose. Without looking around, he walked to the front of the class and accepted the prize from Mr. Walker, said thank you, and returned to his chair.

Mr. Walker, noticing the class' attitude, said, "Remember, this is supposed to be a fun reward to encourage each of you to study your lessons. Don't be upset if you didn't win. Just keep trying."

Mr. Walker lifted the paper and said, "Here are the ten answers that Mr. Jenkins gathered from your papers: Daniel - lived in Jerusalem; was kidnapped; had three friends who were also kidnapped; had no defects; was popular; the king liked him; learned languages; ate God's food; understood dreams, and was better than the magicians. Now, I'll read my four additional answers: Daniel - was intelligent; learned easily; understood science; and was renamed Belteshazzar.

"Next week's Bible Hero lesson is taken from Matthew chapter 14 and is about Peter walking on the water. Do your best to win. Let's close our lesson in prayer."

Alex closed his eyes, but he wasn't praying. He disappointedly asked himself, "Why do I even try?" Of course, he knew why. The bowling passes! He liked when his friends gathered around him asking to be chosen. He wondered silently, "Who will Theodore invite?"

Alex jumped as he heard his name. He looked around and saw that everyone was gone but he and his teacher.

"I hope you brought a pillow and a sandwich with you if you're spending the night," Mr. Walker joked.

Alex pretended to smile as he rose from his chair, planning to leave.

"Where did you get your answers?" Mr. Walker asked. "The Bible didn't tell the color of Daniel's hair or the kind of shoes that he wore."

Alex looked at the floor and frowned. Without looking up he said, "I watched Mom's Bible movie."

"I think you'd do better to read your own Bible," he advised. Mr.

The Dog Was Adopted Too

Walker sat at the table across from where Alex had been. He asked, "Can you stay a minute? I'd like to talk to you."

"I guess so," Alex said as he returned to the table and stood next to the chair where he had been sitting. He sighed and thought, "I'm going to get one lecture at home from Dad, and now I'm getting one at church from Mr. Walker. What a day."

"I've noticed that Theodore hasn't used the passes that he's won," Mr. Walker began. "He's a new kid in our community and I'm worried that he doesn't have any friends. Would you mind helping Theodore become part of your group?"

Mr. Walker couldn't have stunned Alex more if he had whopped him with a wet mop. He wasn't in the mood to be Theodore's friend, now or ever.

He looked down and said, "I never see him because he's always on his way home." Alex shifted his weight from one foot to the other as he stuck his hands into his pockets. He continued, "Besides, I don't know his phone number or his address."

Mr. Walker didn't say anything, so Alex looked up to see if he had been listening. Mr. Walker's eyes looked sad, so Alex added, "I'll try."

The teacher rose from his chair and smiled. He said, "That's all I wanted. Thanks."

Alex walked out of the room followed by Mr. Walker who turned off the lights and closed the door.

Alex left the education building and walked toward the auditorium heading for the worship service. He watched the ground as he kicked pine cones and pieces of paper with the tips of his shoes. He thought about what Mr. Walker had said and wondered why Theodore hadn't been using his bowling passes. He thought, "Maybe he really doesn't have any friends."

Chapter Two
Sunday Afternoon
Startled

The van rolled to a stop in the driveway and Dad turned the engine off. Mom and Leora hurried inside to fix lunch. Alex unbuckled his seat belt and slid his door open.

Dad said, "Wait, I want to talk to you."

Alex sighed, then closed the van door loudly. He sat back folding his arms and waiting for his dad to begin the lecture.

Dad said, "I don't know why you were running in the hall, but you could have seriously injured somebody. We're lucky that your mom was the only one who was hurt."

Alex said, "I'm sorry. I was in a hurry because I was late for the contest. I didn't see Mom or the girls in time to stop."

"Do you think that bowling passes are more important than safety or manners?" Dad asked.

"No, sir," replied Alex with another sigh.

Dad said, "I know you didn't intend to hurt anyone, but you have to learn to think first. Have you noticed that you've been getting crankier every week? I think you're letting the contest take over your thinking. If things don't change, you won't be competing anymore."

Alex complained silently, "Oh, great!"

The Dog Was Adopted Too

"Alex!" said Dad sternly.

Alex looked up at his Dad, trying not to look as aggravated as he felt.

"I think you need to be more mindful of the people around you. I have a book on safety and manners that I want you to read. You'll be grounded until you have finished reading it. If your attitude hasn't improved after reading it, you will continue to be grounded. Come inside. You'll start reading the book as soon as lunch is over."

"Yes, sir," Alex sighed as he got out of the van. He and Dad went inside and saw Mom and Leora carrying food to the table on the patio.

Mom called, "Roger, Alex, bring the chips and hot dogs when you come out."

Alex and his dad carried the food out and placed it on the table. His family was enjoying the picnic atmosphere, but he couldn't get into the mood. He kept wondering how big the book on manners was. He didn't want to be grounded all week. When he wasn't fretting about the book, he worried about having to talk to Theodore.

After lunch was over, the family carried the dishes to the kitchen. Mom and Leora put everything away and went for a walk.

Dad called Alex into the living room and sat on the couch. Alex had no clue what his punishment would be, so with an attitude like a rain cloud, he sat next to his dad.

Dad gave him a book and said, "I want you to read this. Write 10 rules about safety and another 10 rules about manners."

Alex took the book and thumbed through it. He decided that it wouldn't take too long to read, and his attitude improved.

When his dad stood up to leave, Alex said, "Wait, Dad. I need to talk to you for a minute." His dad sat back down. Alex told him about being asked to help Theodore become part of his group of friends.

Dad said, "Well, that's a tall order. What do you think about it?"

Alex fumbled with the book and said, "I don't know. Theodore has been in the class for a while, but he's never talked to any of us. Then, all-of-a-sudden, he started entering the contests and has won every one of them." He looked up and admitted, honestly, "We sort of feel like he's just butting in."

"Do you know anything about Theodore?"

"No sir."

"Your mother heard that he's living with his aunt and uncle because something happened to his parents. Can you imagine how you might feel if you never saw your mom or me again?"

Alex looked up in amazement. He had never thought about why Theodore always seemed to be sad.

Dad said, "Try thinking how you'd feel if you were the new kid in town."

"I always figured that moving would be exciting," replied Alex.

"It might sound exciting, but if you don't want to move, it's not much fun," Dad said.

"You moved a lot when you were a kid, didn't you, Dad?"

"Yes, and I didn't like it."

"Why not?"

"I had to leave all of my friends and start over again at a new school each time I had to move. Mine was only one name for everyone to remember, but I had dozens of names to learn. It always took a while before I felt like I fit in. Often, just about the time I made friends and learned my way around town, my dad would change jobs and we'd move again. I never had life-long friends like you have. You're very blessed."

Alex thought about his closest friends: Michael, Derick, Joshua, and Kevin. He couldn't imagine not seeing them every day.

"Now, Alex, I want you to try thinking about how you would feel if you were the new kid, without friends, and without your parents."

Alex hadn't considered that Theodore might have problems. "What should I do, Dad?"

"It sounds like Mr. Walker has given you a big job. Pray about it and I'll talk to your mom. You know that we'll be glad to help you in any way that we can."

"Thanks Dad," Alex said as he stood up and carried the book to his room. He sat at his desk, thought about Theodore for a while, and said a prayer for him. He looked at the clock and saw that it was 1:30. He picked up the book on manners and began reading. It was hard to concentrate because he could hear other kids talking outside as they walked past his house. He couldn't keep Theodore out of his thoughts and had to keep re-reading sentences each time his thoughts wandered.

He heard giggling from his mom and sister as they entered the house. Their laughter and conversation made him feel lonely and sad. He thought about Theodore being alone, which made him feel worse. He looked at the clock again and saw that it was 4 P.M. He had read

The Dog Was Adopted Too

three chapters in two and a half hours. "What a day," he sighed.

He heard Mom tell Leora to get cleaned up for evening worship. He listened as she walked from room to room looking for the rest of her family. The sound of her footsteps grew louder as she approached his room and said happily, "Get ready for church."

He wasn't looking forward to going back to church tonight. He felt depressed, and he knew that his friends would be teasing him again. There was no way of avoiding it, so he decided to "face the music," as he had heard his parents say when they had to do some dreaded thing. He stood up, stretched his arms, rubbed his eyes, and yawned. He combed his hair, brushed his teeth, and was soon in the van, on his way to church with his family.

Dad parked the van. Alex watched as his parents and Leora exited the vehicle, and the trio walked across the parking lot. His dad held the glass entrance door open to allow his sister, mom, and another family to enter the building.

When the glass entrance door closed, he slid the van door open to get out, but another car pulled into the next parking spot. He quietly pulled the door closed and threw himself down across the seat. He heard the voices of Mr. Walker and his daughter, Ariel, and the sound of their car door closing. He hoped he hadn't been seen. Their voices faded away and when he peaked over the seat, the parking lot was empty once again.

Alex looked around and carefully got out of the vehicle. He bent down low and sneaked around car after car. He felt like a spy in the movies. Crouching behind a truck near the glass entrance door that his family had just gone through, he thought through his plan. He would walk straight and tall into the class, as if nothing mattered, and sit quietly in the back of the room. When class was over, he planned to let everyone leave first, then hurry to the auditorium and sit with his family. After church, he would stay close to his mom and dad. He decided that his friends wouldn't tease him with his parents near.

He looked around, saw no one, and lunged for the entrance. He flattened himself against the wall, then leaned way over and peaked into the building through the glass door. Seeing no one, he breathed a sigh of relief and opened the door quietly. Still seeing no one, he closed the door carefully and tiptoed around the corner toward his classroom.

"Look out!" a voice boomed, "Here he comes! Run for your life!"

Alex jumped back! There, standing before him, were his best friends in the whole world, each one laughing.

"Oh, no!"

"Call 9-1-1!"

"Help, save us!"

For the second time that day, heads were sticking out of classroom doors. He could hear teachers "shushing" their students. He felt his face blush like it was on fire.

Their teacher stepped into the hall and called, "Come to class, boys."

"Some friends you are," said Alex. "You almost gave me a heart attack."

The boys laughed. One patted him on his back and another messed up his hair as he trotted by. Alex relaxed and laughed as he and the boys walked to class. He combed his fingers through his hair as he thought to himself, "So much for a quiet entrance."

He knew the pranks were just a part of life with his friends, and he knew he would have teased them if things had been reversed. He thought, "I sure would miss them if I had to move." He noticed that he felt less depressed.

Later, after class, he met Ariel, Billie, and Susan in the hall and apologized for knocking them down. The girls arrogantly lifted their noses and turned their backs toward him.

Ariel glanced over her shoulder and said, "Go away little boy, you're bothering us." The girls tried to act mad but couldn't keep from laughing. They turned back around and accepted Alex's apology.

Joking with each other, Alex and the girls walked to the auditorium to join their families for the church service. He thought, "I'd even miss these girls if I had to move."

After the singing of the hymns, Pastor Joe began his sermon by reminding everyone about "Praise in the Park" the following Sunday.

He said, "Your assignment is to remember ways that God has blessed your life and share them at the picnic." Whispered blessings were shared like a spring breeze across the congregation.

The church service seemed to fly by, and before he knew it, he was home again. It had been such an emotionally exhausting day. He felt like he had been on a wild and crazy roller coaster ride. After eating supper, everyone went to bed. As he laid quietly, the events of the day played like movie re-runs over and over in his mind. He remembered the embarrassment of running into his mom and her students... He had lost the contest... Theodore had won the contest... and Mr. Walker had asked him to be Theodore's friend. Topping everything else, his dad had grounded him!

"What a day!" He sighed as he thought about Dad's lecture. "Dad had been right," he admitted to himself. All he had been thinking of all week, every week, was winning the contest. Each time he had lost, his bad attitude had made his problems get worse.

Alex had promised to pray about it. "Can't hurt," he had said to Dad.

Alex thought about Theodore's problem. He wondered how well he had known his uncle and aunt before having to move in with them. He wondered if he got sad enough to cry at night. His concern for Theodore began to grow.

He laid his head on his pillow and chuckled as he remembered his friends scaring him. "Those guys must have planned to do that all afternoon," he thought to himself. He knew he had some good friends and thought, "Theodore should have a chance to have good friends like I do."

As he drifted off to sleep, he decided to try harder to remember what is important. He thought to himself, "Tomorrow, after school, I'll work on the contest."

His eyes flew open and he sat up and said aloud, "I will not try to win by watching a movie!" He laid his head back onto the pillow and let sleep take him to the land of restful dreams.

As Alex peacefully slept, God began to grow the seed of concern that He had placed in the boy's heart. Alex didn't know it now, but he was about to learn a lot more than he could ever imagine.

Chapter Three
Monday Morning
The Sound

    Alex arrived at school with the intention of talking to his friends. He didn't know what to say to Theodore, so he planned to avoid him. This turned out not to be a problem since Theodore was nowhere to be seen. He expected to see all of his friends at one time, but they seemed to be scattered. Since he had wanted to talk to all of the guys as a group, he decided that after school he would talk to them at the park.
    Later, as he rode the school bus home, he watched the scenery go by and thought about the things that he had to do when he got home. He organized everything in his mind according to importance. He knew that he would still be grounded until he finished reading the book of manners, so he decided reading would be the first thing to do. Doing homework should be second and doing his chores would be third. He figured that he had just enough time to accomplish his responsibilities before joining his friends at the park to talk to them about Theodore.
    His bus stopped in front of his house and he trotted up the steps and rushed inside. His mom greeted him with a snack, which he gladly accepted. He finished eating, thanked his mom, and hurried to his

room. He finished the book and wrote the rules that Dad was expecting to receive. He finished his homework and his chores, then hurried out to the garage. He gave the papers and the book of manners to his dad, who seemed pleased with his efforts.

Dad asked, "Did you learn anything?"

"I learned to consider other people's feelings first, say 'please' and 'thank you,' and I should be polite. Oh wait, that's the same thing. Also, don't shout or run inside buildings." He closed one eye and looked at the ceiling as he tried to think of something else. Opening both eyes wide he looked at Dad and added, "Oh, yea, don't run into your mom."

Dad added, "Don't run into anyone!"

"I know. I was just kidding," Alex replied with a smile.

"Alright, you aren't grounded anymore," replied Dad, returning Alex's smile.

"May I go to the park? I need to talk to the guys about Theodore."

"Go ahead, but don't be late for supper. Head home when the first street light comes on."

"Thanks, Dad," Alex called over his shoulder as he headed for the door.

Alex hurried from the garage and trotted down the sidewalk, waving at neighbors as he went. He reached the park entrance, and suddenly, a big dog ran by and bumped against his left leg. He fell with a flop, face down onto a pile of freshly mowed grass. He rose up and caught a glimpse of Mr. Norton's brown collie running into the park.

He groaned, "Wally! You silly dog. You've dug another hole under the fence."

Alex rolled over and relaxed. A breeze felt good as it blew strands of his hair around. He closed his eyes and listened. A bee buzzed by, and from the distance, he could hear voices and music. He opened his eyes, looked up, and saw beautiful, fluffy clouds drifting lazily across the bright blue sky. He decided to lie still and enjoy the moment. He and his family enjoyed searching the clouds for fluffy animal shapes. Remembering happy times with his family made him think about Theodore. He took a deep breath and decided to go find his friends.

Just as he sat up, he heard laughter coming from inside the park. He jumped up and ran as curiosity drove him down the long, worn trail that curved between the double rows of hedges. The gazebo came into view, but it was empty. Close to the wooded area, he saw Wally running and bouncing around four boys, two standing and two on the ground. Recognizing Michael, Joshua, Kevin, and Derick, he ran to meet them. As he neared the boys he could see that Michael was holding his sides and laughing. Joshua was on his knees laughing and trying to keep Wally from licking his face each time he bounded by. Kevin was sitting on the ground, rocking back and forth, nearly howling.

Derick, looking serious, was standing with his arms folded and saying, "Very funny. You're such good friends." When he saw Alex walking his way, he said, "Great! I guess you think it was funny, too."

Joshua stood up and asked, "Did you see that?"

"No, what happened?" asked Alex.

"Oh," Michael gasped, "you've got to hear this."

"That's right!" Derick said sarcastically, "Make sure everyone knows! Hey, a car is coming. You want me to flag it down so you can tell those people, too?"

Kevin laughed and said, "Sure, if you don't mind."

Derick frowned and Michael nudged him with his elbow and said, "Oh, come on, grouch. It was funny."

Alex asked, "Guys, would someone please tell me what happened?"

"Okay. I will!" answered Joshua, "Kevin, Michael, and I were waiting for you and Derick when we heard a sound in the bushes. We saw Derick hiding in the shadows. I guess he was planning to scare us. Just then, Wally plunged through the bushes and Derick dove behind a stump."

Michael giggled and said, "He stuck his head up, looked around and started to come our way. Each time he moved, Wally moved behind him. Derick would stop, and Wally would stop."

"Derick sneaked to the edge of the bushes," Kevin said, and broke out into laughter again. "That's when Wally charged toward Derick and chased him."

Michael said, "Wally pounced and tackled him, knocking him to the ground."

"Yeah," Joshua added, "and Derick hollered 'Help!'"

Alex tried to appear serious as he looked at Derick, who was trying to keep from smiling. He asked him, "Why were you running from Wally?"

Trying to sound irritated, Derick said, "I heard this sound, and

The Dog Was Adopted Too

when I looked behind me, all I saw was a big, brown, hairy thing running after me. It scared me half to death and these so-called friends of mine think that's funny."

Alex said, "Well, it must've been funny. You're about to burst out laughing yourself."

"Yea," Derick chuckled and said, "I guess it was. Boy! I'm sure glad it was Wally and not a bear."

"Lions, and tigers, and collies, oh, my!" teased Joshua.

The laughing boys, without much sincerity, apologized to Derick. Soon, the chattering boys, followed by Wally, were strolling around aimlessly until, as always, they ended up inside the gazebo.

Alex leaned against one of the supports and said, "I want to ask all of you something important." When all of the boys were looking at him, he said, "Mr. Walker told me that Theodore doesn't have any friends and asked me to help him become part of our group. I figured it wouldn't hurt for us to try to be his friends."

Michael said, "I don't think he wants friends."

"Yeah," said Joshua. "If he wanted friends, why he is always gone when church or school is over? Why doesn't he hang around and talk with us?"

Derick frowned and said, "He sure messed up our bowling."

Alex said, "I talked to my dad, and he said that something bad had happened to Theodore's family causing him to move in with his aunt and uncle." Alex continued to tell them what his dad had said about being in a new town. He asked, "So, how about it?"

Joshua said, "I guess if that happened to me I'd be in a bad mood, too. Sure, why not?"

"Yeah, it's okay with me," said Derick.

"I'll try," agreed Michael.

"What do you want us to do?" inquired Kevin.

"I'm not sure yet. It's like Joshua said, he goes home as soon as church and school are over. I don't even know where he lives or what his phone number is."

"When you get that figured out, let us know," Joshua said.

"Okay." Alex noticed Wally running around and said, "I've got to take Wally back home. Thanks for the laugh, Derick."

"Any time," Derick chuckled.

Alex called to Wally, "Come here, boy." Expecting to play, the dog sprinted to Alex's side. "Let's go home," Alex said and raced the dog through the park, toward the Norton's house.

Chapter Four
Monday Evening
A Fine Young Man

Alex and Wally rounded the last turn and saw Mr. Norton standing at the fence in his yard, holding the gate open, and calling, "Wally! Wally, come here!" The dog sprinted past Alex, crossed the street, and ran into his yard.

Alex stopped to let a car go by, then walked over to join Mr. Norton who said, "I'm so glad you found him. I was getting worried."

"He was at the park. Would you like for me to fill in the hole that he dug?" Alex asked as he leaned against the fence.

"No, thanks," Mr. Norton replied. "Frances came home from college earlier today, and filled it in. You know, you're the only person around who offers to do things to help me. I appreciate it and one day I'll find a way to repay you."

Alex replied honestly, "I'm glad to help."

"You're a fine young man," Mr. Norton said. "Come on inside for a few minutes and see Frances. She baked a cake. You still like cake, don't you?"

The Dog Was Adopted Too

Alex smiled and said, "Yes, sir, I do!" Mr. Norton closed the gate and guided Alex up the steps to the porch, and into the living room.

Alex always enjoyed visiting Mr. Norton. His house smelled like his grandparent's house. Today, the fragrance of the warm, freshly baked cake greeted him. He inhaled deeply and said, "M-m-m-m." As he exhaled, his stomach growled loudly. He tried to muffle the sound with his hands.

"It sounds like you got here just in time," chuckled Mr. Norton.

Laughing with embarrassment, Alex said, "I think so."

Mr. Norton led the way to the kitchen where they found Wally watching Frances pour milk. When she saw Alex, she smiled and asked, "Will you stay for cake and milk?"

"I've already invited him," said Mr. Norton. "He brought Wally home."

"Thanks, Alex," said Frances. "I wish he wouldn't run off like that. I'm worried that he's going to get hit by a car, and I don't know what to do to stop him."

"I could make him afraid of traffic by chasing him around the yard with the truck," joked Mr. Norton.

"Well, that would teach him to stay away from your truck," snickered Alex.

"Daddy! Alex!" Frances said, pretending to be shocked. "You're both so tender hearted," she said as she placed Alex's milk and cake on the table next to her own and sat down.

Alex chuckled as he sat at the table and took a bite of the cake. "Wow! This tastes better than it smells," he exclaimed.

"Thanks, it's one of my mom's favorite recipes," Frances said, and then asked, "What have you been doing besides rescuing dogs?"

"I go around knocking people over," Alex responded.

Frances and Mr. Norton both looked amazed and said, "What?"

He smiled as he told them about the accident at the church.

"I bet your mom didn't like that very much," laughed Mr. Norton.

"Neither did my dad," admitted Alex.

Frances, trying to hold back her laughter, asked, "Why were you in such a hurry?"

Alex explained, "We were having a contest in Sunday school, and I only had a minute to give my paper to the teacher."

"How did you do?" asked Frances.

"Not too well. Another boy won," said Alex. He snapped his fingers and added, "Oh, I forgot. I've got to get his phone number."

Mr. Norton asked. "Who's number?"

Alex answered, "He is a boy in my Sunday school class. My teacher asked me to introduce him to some of my friends."

Frances said, "That's a good thing to do. I know a boy who doesn't have many friends. I wish he knew someone like you to help him to get to know people."

Alex smiled, finished his snack and wiped the milk mustache from his lip. He said, "Thanks for the cake and the milk. Let me tell you what Wally did at the park."

Frances said, "Oh no. What did he do?"

Crouching down and using his hands along with facial expressions, he told them the story of Wally scaring Derick.

Mr. Norton laughed and said, "That sounds like Wally."

Frances giggled as she patted Wally's head and said, "You're such a stinker."

Wally's eyes sparkled as he licked Frances' hand.

Alex said, "I'd better go before it gets late and I get into trouble."

Mr. Norton said, "We don't want that. Come again. You're always welcome."

Frances, Mr. Norton, and Wally walked with Alex to the porch. The family and their dog watched as Alex crossed the street heading home. As he walked, he thought, "I hope I can remember to get Theodore's phone number when I get home."

As he entered his home, his mother said, "Where have you been? You're late for supper."

Alex said, "I'm sorry. Wally got out of his yard again, and I took him home and visited for a few minutes. Did you know that Frances is home from college?"

Alex's mom said, "I'm glad you could help them, but you have to try to watch your time more carefully."

He said, "Yes, ma'am," and cleaned up for supper. He hurried to the table and found everyone waiting for him to say the prayer. When he sat down he saw that his mom had a cake for dessert. He smiled and thanked God for the good food and both desserts.

After supper his mom reminded him that it was his turn to do the dishes. He had learned a long time ago that complaining only made things worse, so he said, "Okay," and began carrying the dishes to the sink.

When the dishes were washed and put away, he joined his family in the living room. He listened to Dad as he read aloud one of Leora's library books. Alex said, "I've got to read my Bible story. I'll see you in the morning." After goodnight hugs, he bathed and went to his room. He opened his Bible to Matthew 14:22-23 and read, "Immediately Jesus made His disciples get into the boat and go before Him to the other side, while He sent the multitudes away. And when He had sent the multitudes away, He went up on a mountain by Himself to pray. And when evening had come, He was alone there."

Alex put the Bible away and thought to himself, "I guess Jesus got tired, too." He went to bed, and as he fell asleep, he thought about Derick and Wally. If anyone had been watching him, they would have wondered why he was chuckling in his sleep.

Chapter Five
Tuesday Morning
Wally?

At school, Alex searched for Theodore during lunch break and found him sitting alone, reading a book. Their conversation was awkward and before he remembered to ask Theodore for his phone number, the bell had rung, sending them back to their classes. At recess Alex searched for Theodore but couldn't find him. The day rolled on as usual, and when school was over, Theodore was still nowhere to be seen.

After Alex returned home, he found his mom and Leora busy as bees preparing for "Praise in the Park" on Sunday. Dad, as usual, was busy in the garage. Alex ate a snack then did his homework and chores. After checking with Dad, he ran to the park, expecting to see his friends. He waited at the gazebo, their usual meeting place. No one was there, so he decided to wait at the pond.

A parade of fluffy clouds teased Alex with animal shapes. Alex saw an elephant with big ears and a small body. He watched as the trunk drifted away and the ears lengthened into the shape of alligator jaws. It

The Dog Was Adopted Too

now looked like the elephant trunk was going to be gobbled up by an alligator head.

A duck caught Alex's attention as it flew across his line of vision. He followed it with his eyes as it landed in the pond creating expanding rings of ripples. He remembered a night that his family had attended a picnic in the park for a community bonfire. He and some friends had stood near the pond watching the reflections of the moon and the many multi-colored lights dancing on the water. Alex and his friends had watched a family of mallard ducks, swimming in small circles. The ducks were making happy little chuckling sounds, then without warning, one of them would blast out loudly, Quack! Quack! Quack! It sounded just like a great, big belly laugh. Each time a duck "laughed" it made them laugh, too. One friend had said, "It sounds like that duck is the only one who understands the joke." Alex snickered to himself as he remembered that evening.

He scanned the pond, hoping to see another group of ducks but only saw two swimming toward a leaf that had just fallen into the water. One duck plucked it up only to have the other one snatch it from his bill. The pair decided it wasn't food and swam toward another mystery treasure. Alex watched the rippling trails that the two happy ducks were leaving in the smooth surface of the pond. The smell of barbeque on the grill made him feel hungry, and in the distance, he heard the "ping" of a bat as it hit a ball. He closed his eyes, took in a deep breath, and let it out slowly. It was so peaceful that he felt as if he were inside one of his mother's beautiful, musical snow-globes, only without the snow.

Suddenly, the peaceful moment burst when he heard the sound of galloping feet and felt a rush of air from behind him. Alex whirled around and saw a brown streak disappearing down the bike path. He took off running, calling, "Wally!" Under his breath, he muttered, "Another hole under Mr. Norton's fence."

Wally, hearing his name, skidded to a stop, turned and ran back toward Alex who dropped to one knee and said, "Good dog, come here." Wally found a new burst of speed, and as he neared Alex, his size became apparent. Alex opened his eyes wide and said, "That's a big dog." He stood up and held his hands before him intending to block the impact of the dog. The boy expectantly gritted his teeth, scrunched his eyes, and held his breath as he braced himself. Wally adjusted his trajectory and sidestepped just barely missing full impact. The dog brushed heavily against the boy's knee almost knocking him down. Alex regained his balance and said, "What are you doing!" as he exhaled hoarsely. With relief and a new determination, he rocketed after the energetic dog.

Like a skilled baseball player, Wally skidded to a stop and turned, facing his opponent. His eyes sparkled as he lowered his chest to the ground, placed his head between his front paws, and wagged his tail high in the air. He seemed to smile as he watched Alex get nearer, then with a sudden about-face he was off again.

Alex said, "So, we are playing chase." Wally followed the curve of the bike path and disappeared around the turn. Alex remembered the turn formed a wide "U" shape, which almost doubled back on itself, forming a short cut. He had used this almost invisible trail once before during a race. It had placed him far ahead of his friends allowing him to win. He saw the path leading to the short cut. He jumped the shallow ditch and raced through the bushes. Alex jumped over one bush, dodged another, and ran through the last one. He continued down the trail and hopped over the second ditch. He stopped and stood on the main trail looking both ways. He expected to surprise the dog, which he was sure would come running around the curve. He listened, but all he could hear was his own heavy breathing and the sound of his heart pounding in his ears. As he stood still, his heart and breathing got softer and he began hearing a steady rhythm near him. He looked over his shoulder and said, "Oh!" and jumped away. There was Wally, sitting behind him panting like a puffing locomotive. The dog's tongue hung to one side and rapidly curled and uncurled with every breath. Wally pulled in his long tongue, swallowed and let it flop out again as he continued panting.

Alex put his fists on his hips and said, "You scoundrel." Wally lifted his ears and cocked his head to one side as his eyes glistened joyfully.

Alex changed his voice to a sweeter, gentler, "sing-song" tone and said, "Stay, Wally. Be a good boy. Let Alex pet you." Alex slowly reached for the dog. Just as his fingertips almost touched the collar, Wally barked, and in what seemed like one movement, was ten feet down the path. Alex lunged to tackle the dog but missed and slid in the dust. He jumped up and said, "Here we go again."

The race continued up the path until it joined a road which led to the edge of the park where Wally slowed to a stop. He was still in the park but was now across the intersection from his house. Alex stopped running and walked wearily toward the heavily panting collie. He dropped to his knees and stroked the dog's head. He huffed and puffed as he rested, trying to catch his breath. After a minute, he said, "You were going home anyway weren't you?" He stood up and told the dog, "Come on. Let me take you to your yard." He reached down toward Wally's collar. The dog suddenly jumped around again and ran into the street.

It all happened so suddenly that Alex just watched the car go by, wondering why it was going so fast. Then he heard Wally's cries. Alex looked back to see the dog thrashing about on the pavement as he was trying to get up. Alex shouted, "Oh, no!" and ran to Wally who was struggling and screaming painfully with every movement. The boy had never seen anything so awful. He knelt by the dog, then saw a pickup truck approaching. He waved his arms over his head to make sure the driver saw them. The man drove around the boy and dog, stopped nearby, and quickly getting out of the truck, ran back toward them.

Alex said, "It's going to be alright, boy." He put his hand on Wally, who yelped and bit him, sinking a long canine tooth deep into Alex's palm. The startled boy jumped back and grabbed his hand.

The man said, "Stay away from the dog," and ran back to his truck. He returned carrying a towel and wrapped it over and around Wally's head. Alex saw the man read Wally's rabies tag and say, "Good, he's had his shots."

Alex held the howling, towel-wrapped dog, trying to calm him. He could see blood on the pavement but couldn't tell where it was coming from.

The man asked, "Is this your dog?"

Using his uninjured hand, Alex pointed toward Mr. Norton's house and said, "No, he lives there."

The man sprinted to his truck, backed it up, and stopped next to the struggling pair. From the bed of his truck, he pulled out a piece of plywood and said, "Lift up the dog's head."

Alex lifted Wally's head. The dog howled with pain as the man pushed and slid the plywood sheet under him. Alex and the man lifted the heavy, makeshift stretcher to the tailgate of the truck and pushed it in. Alex jumped up and sat next to Wally. He tried to hold Wally still as the man turned the truck around, drove across the intersection, and parked next to Mr. Norton's truck in the driveway.

Having heard the commotion, Mr. Norton was looking out the door of his house to see what had happened.

"Mr. Norton! Wally's been hit by a car!" Alex shouted from the bed of the truck.

"Frances!" Mr. Norton cried out to his daughter as he hurried down the steps. He sprinted to the gate and fumbled with the latch. Frances ran to help her dad open the lock and swung the gate open.

The two men and Frances spoke briefly. Frances ran to the truck to be with Wally and sat next to Alex. Over the cries of the dog Alex heard Mr. Norton shout, "Put him in my truck!" Alex hopped down and trotted to the near-by truck, tugged on the latch and let the tailgate down. The men lifted the plywood stretcher, hauled the heavy dog from the truck and placed him in the bed of Mr. Norton's truck. Frances jumped up into the bed of her truck and sat next to Wally, trying to comfort him as he continued to cry. Alex closed the tailgate and stepped aside. He saw Frances wiping tears as she spoke to Wally.

Mr. Norton thanked the man as he backed his truck out of the yard, then he hurriedly drove down the street. Alex walked from the driveway and stood in the street watching the truck drive away. The man closed Mr. Norton's gate and walked to Alex's side.

Alex, unaware of the man's presence, felt confused and stood with his arms hanging by his side, as he silently watched the truck disappear around the turn. Wally's cries could no longer be heard. Suddenly, the chaos was over and silence loomed in the air. Alex couldn't have felt lonelier even if he had been God's only creation.

Chapter Six
Tuesday Afternoon
The Emergency

The man with the pick-up looked over at Alex and saw how devastated he was. He intended to speak words of comfort to the boy, but what he saw made him speechless. Alex was standing next to a puddle of blood on the street. The man lifted Alex's bleeding right hand and said, "Let me take a look at that."

Alex, thinking that he was alone, jumped and pulled away at the man's touch. The sudden movement made his hand throb. The ordeal of the accident had numbed his thoughts, and he just stood watching the blood drip from his hand and fingers to the ground.

Holding Alex's hand, the man took a handkerchief from his pocket and wiped the blood away to reveal the dark, bleeding hole left by Wally's fang. He wrapped the cloth tightly and said worriedly, "Let me take you home."

Alex noticed that the man's voice sounded familiar. Rousing from his confusion, he recognized his Sunday school teacher. Alex followed Mr. Walker and climbed into the truck. Mr. Walker made a phone call as he drove. Alex somberly stared out of the window as he thought of Wally. The image of the dog thrashing about in the street kept replaying in his mind as tears ran down his face.

Mr. Walker's voice distracted Alex's thoughts. He said, "Hello, Rebecca, this is Howard. I'm bringing Alex home. A dog bit him and his hand is bleeding...Yes, and the dog has a current rabies tag... We'll be there in a few minutes...Yes. Bye."

Alex wiped his eyes and asked, "Where did they take Wally?"

"Mr. Norton was taking him to the veterinary hospital," replied Mr. Walker.

"I saw blood on the road," said Alex with a worried sound in his voice. "How bad was he hurt?"

"I didn't see any blood on the dog," replied Mr. Walker. "All of that blood came from you. That's why I'm concerned about your hand. I just called your mom and she's waiting for us at your house. We're almost there."

Mr. Walker parked his truck in Alex's driveway. Alex's mom came out and met them. She gasped when she saw the blood-drenched handkerchief and so much blood on Alex's pants. She peeked under the cloth, then took Alex inside as Mr. Walker ran to get Alex's dad. Mom had called the nurse by the time the men ran inside the house.

She hung up the phone and said, "We need to take him to the emergency room."

"I'll move my truck," said Mr. Walker. "Let me know what the doctor says."

Dad led Alex to the van. Mom called their neighbor, Mrs. Bonnie, who agreed to let Leora stay with her while they went to the hospital. Leora was disappointed, but went next door where Mrs. Bonnie was waiting, holding the door open for her.

Mom grabbed a fresh towel and slid into the bench seat of the van next to Alex as Dad drove quickly to the hospital.

Mom wrapped the clean towel around his hand, and holding it tightly asked, "What dog bit you?"

"It was Wally," he answered. "A car hit him and he bit me when I tried to help him."

The Dog Was Adopted Too

Alex and his mom swayed each time that his dad put on the brakes or drove around a corner. Alex slid across the seat away from his mom. She pulled him back toward her and buckled his seat belt then buckled her own. Dad slowed as he turned the final corner by the emergency entrance sign. Alex had never been taken to the emergency room before. He felt a chill as he saw attendants removing a patient from an ambulance which was parked by the emergency room doors.

Mom looked out of the window to see what had caught Alex's attention. She saw the activity of the ambulance personnel and put her arm around her son.

She asked, "Are you feeling okay?"

He said, "Yes, ma'am."

As his dad parked the van, Alex asked, "Dad, can we check on Wally, first?"

Dad turned around in his seat and said, "We need to take care of you first. Let's pray before we go inside." Dad said, "Dear God, please guide the doctor and the veterinarian as they take care of Alex and Wally. Help Alex to feel calm and to know how much You love him. I pray in Jesus' name. Amen."

Alex could feel that God was near him and was sure that He was with Wally, too. With his parent's help, Alex got out of the van and walked quickly toward the emergency room. A man in a tan vest pointed toward a cubical where a nurse was waiting. A sign on the door read "triage."

He pronounced, "Try-age."

Mom said, "It is pronounced 'tree-azh'. It's where someone decides who needs to see the doctor first."

The three, guided by the tan vested man, walked into the small room and Alex sat down in the chair that the nurse pulled out for him.

She said, "My name is Ms. Claudia. Let me look at your hand. She removed the bloody towel. Alex could see that the bleeding had slowed down. Ms. Claudia wrapped a fresh cloth around the wound. She put the blood-soaked towel in a plastic bag, gave it to Alex's mom and said, "Go to the waiting room. Your name will be called soon."

After thanking Ms. Claudia, Alex and his parents went to the waiting room. Alex and his mom sat down while his dad went to the vending machines to buy cold drinks.

A female voice called, "Alex Foster," and his mom went to another cubical to fill out the necessary paper work.

Dad returned with the drinks, sat next to his son and asked, "Where's your mom?"

Alex took the cold drink that his dad had opened for him. He sipped the drink, then said, "She's over there," and pointed with the can in his hand.

Alex looked around the room and saw three small groups of people sitting in chairs that were lined against the walls around the room. In the first group, a man sat with his foot resting in another chair. His swollen ankle was blue and his shoes were muddy. In the second group, a woman was holding an icepack against her right eye. In the third group, a little red-faced girl, with her eyes closed, leaned against a lady, maybe her mother. The girl looked as if she had been crying. As the woman stroked the girl's hair, she whispered to her. The girl nodded without opening her eyes.

Alex finished his cold drink and sat the can on a table that was covered with magazines and books. He picked up a magazine and Dad helped him turn the pages. His hand started to ache again so he re-wrapped the towel. He squeezed his hand tightly as he began to watch the waiting room activity again. A lady in a blue uniform opened a door and called out a name. One of the groups of people followed her inside. While the door was open, Alex could see down a long hall with many doors that had a light above each one. People in uniforms busily moved in and out of the rooms. The door closed, and he continued to look at the magazine.

As Alex waited, he watched each of the other groups go through the door. He knew he would be next and felt a little nervous. He went to the water fountain and just as he returned to his chair, the blue uniformed lady opened the door and called his name. He felt butterflies in his stomach as his parents led him through the door and down the long hall. He heard voices coming from almost every room they passed. He also heard a baby crying from somewhere. The lady opened a door which led them into a small room with a bed, chairs, and many strange looking furnishings. A nurse walked in and helped him up onto the bed, unwrapped his hand and inspected it. She mixed some smelly brownish liquid with water in a bowl and used it to clean the wound. She told Alex to soak his hand in the liquid until the doctor came in. She picked

The Dog Was Adopted Too

up the used materials and smiled at Alex as she left the room. After a few minutes, a young man with a wheel chair entered the room.

He said "Hi. I'm Korvyn. I'm going to take you to the x-ray room." He removed Alex's hand from the water, wrapped a towel around it and helped Alex down from the table and into the wheel chair. Without warning, Korvyn spun the chair around and whisked away. About twenty minutes later Korvyn and Alex returned to the room. Korvyn removed the towel and lowered Alex's hand into the water. He told Alex to continue soaking it until the doctor showed up. Korvyn pushed the chair into the hall and walked away.

Alex said, "Korvyn should be a race car driver." Alex's parents laughed as he told them about his x-ray room adventure.

He said, "After hurrying so fast, I had to wait. Several people were sitting in chairs that were lined against the wall. Korvyn waited a few minutes then said, 'I have to go but I'll be back.' He helped me out of the wheel chair onto one of the seats and rolled the chair down the hall.

"Soon my name was called and I went into a room. I had to lay my hand in three different positions under the x-ray machine. A lady in a white lab coat took the pictures. The x-ray machine made a light shine on my hand and made strange sounds. The lady helped me back out to my chair.

"A few minutes later Korvyn came back and loaded me up in the wheel chair again. He raced me down the hall and I asked him why he was going so fast. He said he was a volunteer and was the man-in-demand. He called himself a chariot driver. I told him that I just got grounded for running in the hall at church. He ignored me and turned down a hall then went through a set of double doors. He went so fast that my hair was blowing in the wind. Just before he got to the next hall he pushed the chair sideways. The chair drifted around the corner and almost ran into a man who was carrying a baby. Korvyn went around the man and almost turned me and the chair over. He stopped and grabbed the man who was running backward while trying not to drop the baby. When the man stopped, he looked at Korvyn's name tag. Alex lowered his voice and copied the man, 'Humph. Your name is Korvyn.' Korvyn apologized to the man and brought me back here, but he pushed me a lot slower. He said he didn't want to find out if volunteers can be fired?"

Alex stopped talking and listened to an announcement from a speaker on the wall. A stern sounding woman's voice said, "Korvyn, come to the nurse's station."

Alex and his parents groaned at the same time. His dad said, "Well, I guess he's going to learn if volunteers can get fired. He could have hurt you, the man, and the baby."

Mom said, "I guess he'll learn a lesson about safety and manners."

"I guess I need to loan him your book, Dad," Alex and his parents burst out in laughter.

Running out of things to talk about, Alex and his parents sat silently and looked around the room. His dad stood up and stretched.

He said, "I wonder where the doctor is?" He walked to the door and started to peek out just as it swung open. The door almost hit him in the head and he jumped back.

The doctor, followed by a nurse, came into the room. He said, "Hi. I'm Doctor David Evergood." The nurse looked through some cabinets and drawers and gave bandages and medicine to the doctor as he spoke. The doctor showed Alex and his parents the x-rays and said, "Nothing is broken. Your hand should heal nicely if you don't use it too much for the next few days."

Alex watched as Dr. Evergood checked his wound. Satisfied with what he saw, the doctor wrapped fresh bandages around Alex's hand and between each finger several times. He gently smoothed the rough edges of the taped bandages and asked, "Can you move your fingers?"

"Not too much," Alex replied.

"Good, you don't need to move them much. Does it hurt?" Dr. Evergood asked.

"Yes, a little," Alex admitted.

"I'll give you something to make it feel better," said the doctor. He spoke to the nurse then gave Alex's mom the remaining bandages and the used roll of white tape. "Make an appointment with his regular doctor and follow his orders."

Mom thanked Doctor Evergood, who patted Alex on the back and said, "Watch where you put your hands."

Alex smiled and said, "I'll try."

After the doctor left the room, the nurse said, "I'm Nurse Chris, and I have some medicine for you." He gave Alex a cup of water with some pills and picked up a needle. Alex swallowed the pills, and then

The Dog Was Adopted Too

tightly closed his eyes as he was given an injection. Nurse Chris put a band-aid on Alex's arm and helped him get off the bed. He led Alex and his parents down the hall toward the exit. Nurses and aides smiled and wished them well.

Mom once again sat by Alex in the van on the ride home. Alex rubbed the bandages and said, "They sure are tight."

Dad said, "The doctor didn't want you to be moving your fingers."

Alex said, "Not much chance of that." Alex looked at both sides of his bandaged hand and said, "The bandages make my hand look like a paddle with fingertips sticking out of it." He started feeling tired, leaned his head on his mom's shoulder, and was soon asleep.

When Dad drove the van into the driveway, Leora ran from Mrs. Bonnie's house and greeted them. Alex woke up and walked unsteadily as his parents helped him out of the van, into the house, and to the living room couch.

Leora began asking about the hospital trip. Sleepily Alex said, "We went to triage... Rode in a wheel...Shot from nurse..." Alex's eyes gradually closed as he spoke and soon he was asleep again.

With a look of surprise, Leora asked, "What'd he say about trees and wheels? And who got shot?"

Mom chuckled and pulled Leora close to her. She smiled and said, "Alex needs to rest. You can ask questions later. Come tell me about your visit with Mrs. Bonnie while I fix a snack."

Dad covered Alex, Mom turned off the light, and Leora followed them to the kitchen.

Alex looked deceptively peaceful but in his frantic dreams, he ran calling, "Wally! Stop!"

Chapter Seven
Tuesday Evening
It's Not Your Fault

A stinging feeling in Alex's hand woke him up. He was surprised to find himself on the couch until he looked at his hand and remembered the hospital visit. He asked himself softly, "Did I sleep here all night?" He moved the sheet back and sat up.

He looked at his aching, gauze-wrapped hand. He moved his arm around and discovered that when he held it up, his hand didn't hurt so badly. He held it above his head, until his arm got tired. He rested his arm across the top of his head, but felt silly. Holding his right hand with his left hand above his head made him feel like he was cheering.

The Dog Was Adopted Too

Finally, he stacked two throw pillows on the arm of the couch and placed his hand on top of them. It felt so much better that he didn't want to move.

He relaxed and closed his eyes. Soon he was bored. He picked his head up and looked around the room trying to find something to occupy his time. To his surprise, he noticed Mom and Leora sitting quietly across the room watching him. Feeling a little embarrassed about being watched, he sat back and pretended to straighten his bandages. He asked, "How long have you been sitting there?"

"A little before you woke up," answered Mom.

Alex smirked and rubbed his eyes with his good hand, trying to hide his embarrassment.

Leora asked, "Does it hurt?"

"Not too much," Alex replied. "If I don't hold it high enough, it feels like it is thumping."

"What's making it do that?" Leora asked with her eyes wide open in surprise.

Mom answered, "He's feeling his pulse. Each time that his heart beats, it makes his hand throb and hurt. When he holds it above the level of his heart, it doesn't throb so hard."

Alex looked at his bandaged hand and said, "Well, I'll be glad when it stops." He noticed that he still had blood under one fingernail and scratched at it. His dad came into the room and sat down beside him. He reached over, patted Alex's knee, and asked, "Are you feeling better?"

Alex, checking for blood on his other fingernails, said, "I guess so."

Leora asked, "What happened?"

Alex explained how he'd been in the park running after Wally, trying to take him back home. He told about Wally stopping across the street from Mr. Norton's house. He lifted his hand as if grabbing for the dog's collar. He felt his throat tighten and he swallowed hard trying not to cry.

He said, "Dad, I almost had him. It all happened so fast. The car came out of nowhere and just flew by. And Wally..." Alex's chin quivered and he covered his mouth with his left hand and wiped away a tear with his bandaged right hand.

Dad rubbed Alex's shoulder and said, "Sometimes things are just out of our control, son. Wally was just being a dog and was playing. It was just an accident."

Alex asked, "But why did he bite me? I was only trying to help him." Alex let his head drop against the back of the couch and stared at the ceiling as hot tears ran down his cheeks and onto his neck.

"Injured dogs sometimes snap at anything that touches them," replied Dad.

"Alex, you told me that everything was so confusing that you didn't recognize Mr. Walker until everything was over," Mom reasoned. "I'm sure that Wally was confused too and wouldn't have hurt you under ordinary circumstances. I'm sure that when you see him again, he'll be the same old Wally that he's always been."

The living room was quiet for several minutes. Alex sat up and asked, "May I go visit Wally now?"

Dad replied, "Let's wait until tomorrow. By then Mr. Norton will know more about Wally's condition. He and Mr. Norton probably need some quiet time to rest after such a big evening."

Alex sat back and began inspecting his other fingernails. He wiped away new tears.

"Alex, is there something else bothering you?" Mom asked.

"Well," he began, "when Mr. Walker and I got out of the truck at Mr. Norton's house, everyone talked to each other but ignored me. Wally was put into the truck and Mr. Norton and Frances just drove off and left, like I wasn't even there. Mr. Norton probably blames me for the accident. He must really hate me."

"Oh, Alex!" Mom said as she crossed the room to sit next to him. She put her arm around him and said, "I don't think Mr. Norton blames you. He just had to get Wally to the vet and didn't have time to talk."

Dad whispered to his wife, "I'm going to call Mr. Norton." She nodded and Dad left the room.

Alex wiped his eyes and said, "My hand is starting to hurt worse."

Mom looked at the clock and said, "It's time for another pill. The pain medicine that you were given at the hospital must be wearing off."

She went to the kitchen and heard her husband say, "That's good. Alex thinks you blame him for Wally getting hurt ... Would you mind telling him that yourself? ... Thanks. Let me put him on the phone."

Dad took the phone to Alex, closely followed by Mom, who was carrying the pills and a glass of water. Dad said, "I called Mr. Norton and he'd like to talk to you."

Alex said, "Thanks, Dad." He took the phone and said, "Hello."

Mr. Norton said, "Alex, the veterinarian said that Wally has a cracked rib but that he is going to be fine. He told me that it would take time for him to heal. He needs to stay overnight with the vet, and I'll probably be able to pick him up tomorrow."

Alex was disappointed that he couldn't see Wally now. He nodded and said softly, "Okay."

"Your dad said that you were bringing Wally home when he ran away from you," said Mr. Norton.

"Yes, sir," replied Alex

"He sometimes runs from me, too. Alex, I'm not mad at you. I know it wasn't your fault."

Alex gave a half smile and said, "I was just trying to help."

Mr. Norton added, "I know you were. Remember I said you were the only one who offers to help me?"

"Yes, sir," Alex smiled. He looked up at his dad and answering Mr. Norton, he said, "I remember."

"Well, I meant it. Alex, you're a fine young man," Mr. Norton said with assurance.

He smiled and looked at his mom and said, "Thank you."

"I'm sorry that Wally bit you. How is your hand?" Mr. Norton asked.

"It hurts a little, but the doctor said that I'm going to be alright, too," replied Alex.

Mr. Norton said, "It looks like both of you are going to be fine."

"Yes, sir," Alex replied, smiling again.

"I'll let you know when Wally can have visitors. Call anytime and thanks for your help."

"You're welcome," replied Alex.

"I'll talk to you later," Mr. Norton promised.

Alex said, "Okay. Bye." He handed the phone to his dad and said, "Mr. Norton isn't mad at me. He said that he'd call me when I can visit Wally. Thanks, Dad."

"You're welcome. Do you feel better, now?" he asked.

"I sure do," Alex said.

"Can I go with you when you visit Wally?" Leora asked.

Alex answered, "We'll have to wait to see what Mr. Norton says."

"Here's your medicine," Mom said as she gave Alex the pill and water.

After taking the medicine, he returned the glass and said, "Thanks, Mom."

Leora said, "I would have been really scared at the hospital. Were you scared? Did you try to run away? I would have. Did you cry when you got the shot? I would have. Did the nurse …"

Dad laughed and said, "Leora, slow down and ask one question at a time. Give him a chance to answer."

"I was a little scared, but I didn't try to run away," Alex said. "Dad prayed with me, and everyone at the hospital was nice."

The answers seemed to satisfy Leora. Alex could tell that his little sister was worried. She aggravated him sometimes, but today he could tell that she loves him. He felt tired and lay back down on the couch.

Alex felt a hand on his shoulder and awoke to his dad's voice asking, "Are you hungry?" Alex followed Dad to the dining room and sat down.

His plate was already served with meatloaf, whole kernel corn, and mashed potatoes. He reached for his fork with his bandaged hand and felt the soreness awaken in his palm. He took the fork with his left hand, but each time he tried to scoop the food into his mouth it fell onto his lap. He gave up and laid the fork back down.

Mom said, "I'll make you a sandwich." She took his plate to the kitchen and returned shortly with a meatloaf sandwich.

He thanked her, took a small bite, and chewed slowly. He sipped the milk and put the glass back on the table. He sighed and said, "What an awful day." He sat quietly staring at the glass of milk.

"Are you ready to go to bed?" Mom asked.

Alex nodded his head and walked slowly to his room. He lay down, planning to change his clothes. However, soon he was sound asleep.

Dad was on his way to bed when he saw the light shining from Alex's room. Finding him still dressed he removed the shoes from his son's feet and covered him. He heard Alex mumble something and leaned closer trying to hear.

The Dog Was Adopted Too

Alex said, "Wally!" and tears ran from his closed eyes. Dad laid his hand on Alex's head and said a silent prayer for his troubled son. He gently brushed his fingers through Alex's hair, walked quietly across the room, and turned off the light as he eased the door closed.

Chapter Eight
Wednesday Morning
An Out Of Season Fire

Alex awoke, stretched and rubbed his eyes. Bop! He batted himself on his right eye with his bandaged hand. He rubbed his eye and said, "I could give myself a black eye with this thing." Looking beyond his bandages, he saw the clock glaring at him. He groaned "9:14! I'm late!" He threw the covers back and grumbled, "And, I slept in my clothes." He jumped out of bed and ran to his closet.

Getting undressed was a struggle, but getting dressed was worse. His bulky bandaged hand didn't seem to want to go through the sleeve of his fresh shirt without breaking off a fingertip. After pulling his shirt and pants on, he looked at himself in the mirror. He said, "Now for the buttons and the zipper," He soon learned that, whether you are left or right handed, buttons and zippers were not meant to be one-handed operations. He held his shirt against his chest with his bandaged hand. He used the thumb and two fingers of his left hand to force each rebellious button through its "tight-lipped" button hole. When he was finally through, he shook his aching hand. He looked down and noticed his bare feet.

He moaned, "Oh man!"

He gathered his socks and shoes and sat on the side of his bed. His unruly toes refused to go into his sock all at the same time. He lifted his feet and looked at his crooked socks. One at a time he turned each one until the heels of the socks matched the heels of his feet.

He sighed and said, "I guess that'll work." He stuffed his feet into his shoes and was glad that they didn't have any strings. Taking a quick glance at the mirror he said, "Finally," and trotted to the bathroom.

Brushing his teeth was another learning experience. He opened the toothpaste by biting the lid and turning the tube with his left hand. He placed the toothbrush on the counter with the tube opening on the bristles. Holding the toothbrush down with the fingers of his bandaged hand, he mashed the tube with his left hand and almost buried his toothbrush.

He fumed, "Look at that!" He smeared away most of the toothpaste. With his left hand, which he seldom used, he managed to brush his lips, chin, and a few teeth. He stared at the toothbrush as he thought of another plan of attack.

He said, "Okay," and lifted the toothbrush to his mouth again. Pressing the bristles against his teeth and wagging his head back and forth, he managed to clean almost every tooth. He wiped up the toothpaste and hurried to the kitchen.

He said, "Mom, I'm sorry I didn't get up."

She placed a bowl of cereal and milk on the table and replied, "I let you sleep late," she chuckled. Pointing at his shirt, she said, "Look." Alex watched as she wiped away an unused glob of toothpaste.

"You wouldn't believe the trouble that I've been having. It's kind of hard brushing your teeth with only one hand. You need to try buttons and zippers with only one hand." He plopped himself down in the chair at the table. He said, "I feel tired from all the work I've done just dressing." He looked at the bowl of cereal that his mom had placed before him and sighed. He lifted his spoon with his left hand and leaned over the bowl. After a couple of mishaps and dribbling milk down his chin, he put a spoonful of cereal into his mouth without messing up his clothes.

He looked at his right hand and said, "I'm having problems doing everything because of these bandages. I'll be so glad when they're gone."

"I'm sure you will," Mom said, then added, "You have a doctor's appointment tomorrow."

"Good," Alex said. He lifted his bandaged hand and said, "It's starting to hurt, again."

"I'll get your medicine," Mom said as she went to the cabinet.

Alex took his pill, and after finishing the cereal, went into the living room and lay on the couch. He rubbed the bulky bandage and stared at the TV, which wasn't turned on. He couldn't remember a day when he had felt so clumsy and dreary. He thought that being with his friends would cheer him up, so he planned to go to the park when school was over. The house was quiet without Leora's chatter. The room seemed to grow darker and gloomier with each passing minute. The quietness lulled him to sleep.

The sound of a slamming door made Alex awaken with a jump. Leora was home! The clock told him he had slept for almost five hours.

He noticed that his hand wasn't hurting and said, "Great! I can go to the park, now." After eating a late lunch, he promised, several times, to be careful. Mom drove him to the park gazebo, said she would pick him up in an hour, and drove toward home.

Alex looked around but didn't see even one of his friends. He walked over to a bench, laid down and looked at the sky. There were no fluffy clouds to cheer him. In fact, he thought that the gloomy gray clouds looked a lot like the way he felt. He was thinking about Wally when he saw Theodore walking past.

He sat up and called out, "Theodore, wait a minute."

Theodore turned to see who had called him. He saw Alex approaching and was curious about the white thing on his hand. He trotted and met him half way.

Alex said, "I want to talk to you."

Seeing that the white thing on Alex's hand was bandages, he asked, "What happened?"

Lifting his bandaged hand, Alex said "A dog bit me," then explained about the accident.

Theodore looked concerned as he listened then said, "That's awful!" He lightly rubbed Alex's bandages and said, "It looks like a paddle with fingers."

"I thought so, too," chuckled Alex.

Suddenly, both boys were splattered by water! They flinched and looked around to see who had thrown water on them. A roar over took them and the boys felt like they were standing under a waterfall. The frantic duo dashed for cover in the near-by gazebo, ran up the steps, and stood looking at each other as water dripped from their hair and clothes. A clap of thunder shook the structure and both boys jumped and began laughing at each other. The rain pounded on the roof so heavily that shouting was the only way to be heard.

Theodore wiped his face on his t-shirt and shouted, "I'd call that a cloud burst." The cool wind and their wet shirts made both boys shiver.

Alex shouted, "I'm freezing! Let's sit with our backs together while we wait for the rain to stop."

Each boy sat on the floor and scooted backward until their backs touched. Theodore pulled his knees toward his chest for extra warmth and wrapped his arms around himself as tightly as he could. He briskly rubbed his arms trying to generate heat. The gusts of wind kept blowing light sheets of mist on them.

He said loudly, "I wish this gazebo had solid walls."

Alex copied Theodore and briskly rubbed his arms from his shoulders to his elbows trying to get warm. "Yes," he replied, "and a couple of quilts and a heater would be nice too."

Theodore chuckled then shouted, "Those boys at church sure gave you a hard time. You took their teasing pretty well."

"They're good guys," Alex shouted back. "I've known most of them all of my life and I've teased them, too."

Theodore shivered and shouted through chattering teeth, "I hope the rain stops soon. No one knows where I am, and I'm ready to go home."

Loudly, Alex said, "That's not good. My mom is supposed to pick me up in about a half hour." Alex started to ask where Theodore lived when he saw his dad's truck. Both boys jumped to their feet and watched as Mr. Foster got out of the truck. Holding an umbrella over his head and another one folded in his hand, Alex's dad trotted up the steps to join the two shivering boys.

He gave Alex a folded umbrella and shouted, "Sorry, I don't have another one. I didn't know you had company."

With a trembling voice, Alex shouted, "Thanks, Dad. Theodore and I can share this one. Can we hurry home? We're cold!"

Mr. Foster turned and called out, "Wait for my signal." He ran down the steps holding the opened umbrella closely over his head and jumped into the truck. His left shoulder and leg got soaked as he closed the umbrella and shut the door. He turned on the truck's heater then flashed the headlights.

Theodore opened the umbrella and held the handle. Alex put his bandaged hand under his shirt and gripped the umbrella handle above Theodore's hand.

Both boys shouted, "3 – 2 –1– Go!" The boys almost fell as they ran down the steps tripping over each other's feet. Theodore opened the truck door and let Alex climb up on the slippery leather seat then squeezed in after him. The rain poured in on Theodore until he slammed the truck door. He pulled the umbrella closed and it squeezed water onto his and Alex's pants and shoes. He dropped it to the floor of the truck and tried to wipe the icy water from his clothes.

Mr. Foster asked, "What kind of dance were you two boys doing when you were running down the steps?"

Theodore laughed and said, "That was the umbrella shuffle." Mr. Foster and Alex laughed as Theodore fastened his seat belt first, and then helped Alex buckle his.

Alex hadn't known that Theodore had a sense of humor and the surprise made him laugh harder.

Mr. Foster said, "That was a good one!" He reached across in front of Alex and gave Theodore a high five.

Mr. Foster drove from the park. When the laughter from Theodore's joke settled down, he said, "Theodore, let me take you to our house and you can call your family from there. I'll take you home when the rain slacks up."

Theodore said, "That sounds good to me." He and Alex shivered as Mr. Foster drove home.

Soon the truck pulled into the driveway and both truck doors flew open at the same moment. Two umbrellas popped out, looking like up-side-down tulips dancing toward the porch. Mom opened the door and gave each one a towel. After drying most of the water from themselves, Dad opened the house door and allowed his wife and the two shivering boys to enter before closing the door behind himself.

Mr. Foster said, "Call home and let your aunt and uncle know where you are. Ask if they will let you stay with us until the rain lets up."

Theodore wrapped the towel around his shoulders and phoned home. He grinned widely and excitedly said, "Thanks!" then hung up. He turned around and said, "Uncle Samuel said I can stay, and he told me to have fun."

Alex cheered as he handed his dad another piece of fire wood.

Mom told Alex, "Change your clothes and let Theodore borrow some of your dry clothes to wear."

The boys went to Alex's bed room and soon emerged, still cold but in dry clothes. Theodore stopped and rolled up the pants legs. He told Alex, "You have long legs."

"Sure I do. That's how my feet reach the floor," chuckled Alex.

Alex and Theodore were still laughing at Alex's joke when they joined the others in the living room.

Mom served everyone mugs of hot chocolate, as Dad rubbed his hands together before an out-of-season fire in the fireplace. Mom, Leora, and the three defrosting adventurers sat on cushions in front of the glowing flames. Soon Alex, Theodore and Dad, who were sitting closest to the fire, quit shivering, and one-by-one, moved back away from the heat and formed a semicircle that included Mrs. Foster and Leora. Everyone enjoyed eating popcorn, sipping the chocolate and laughing as each had a story to tell about the unexpected rain.

Alex said, "We felt like popsicles."

Theodore chuckled and said, "Yeah, the kind that has two in a pack."

Dad laughed and said, "You two boys were sitting back-to-back and looked like book ends with no books between you."

Leora said, "I was with Mrs. Bonnie when the rain started. She gave me a garbage bag that she had cut three holes in the bottom. I stuck my head and arms through the holes and wore the bag like a dress. When I ran home, my shoes got so wet that water bubbled out of them." She raised her feet up and said, "Look at my wrinkled toes!"

Everyone laughed as Mom whispered sharply, "Leora!" and pushed her feet to the floor.

Mom said, "I wasn't expecting the rain and had opened all of the windows to let the house air out. When the rain began, I had to run room-to-room closing them. I heard your dad run inside calling me and I kept shouting, 'I'm here! I'm here!' His problem was that he couldn't keep up with me."

Alex laughed as he patted his dad on the shoulder and said, "Poor thing."

Dad laughed and said, "I felt like she was playing hide-and-seek!"

Theodore looked around at Alex's family and remembered fun times with his own family. He asked, "May I tell you something funny that happened to me and my family in a rain storm?"

"Sure!" Mom and Dad said together.

Theodore began his story, "We went camping in the mountains one summer and walked up a tall hill to see a waterfall. On our way back down the trail, it started to rain. It was really weird, because we could hear the rain drops falling on the trees over our heads, but we weren't getting wet. It was a few minutes before the rain drops worked their way through the leaves to drip down on us. Mom and Dad were walking too slowly to suit us, so Ronnie and I ran down to the truck to get out of the rain. Would you believe that the truck was locked? We ran back up the trail, got the keys from Dad, then ran back and waited for them. I cranked the truck and turned on the heater. The windows fogged up and we couldn't see through them. We made circles as we wiped away the haze from the glass and were able to watch for our parents. They took a long time to get to us and were really wet and cold when they finally got in the truck. When Dad drove into our camping site Mom's voice was shaking and she was shivering.

"She said, 'I'm freezing. I can't wait to jump into my warm, dry quilt!' She ran from the truck and into the tent. We followed her, but before we got to the tent we heard a funny squishing sound and then Mom's squealing. We quickly followed dad inside and saw Mom getting up from the floor. She had water dripping from her and she was trying to wipe it from her arms, hair and clothes.

"Her teeth chattered and she groaned, 'The tent must have sprung a leak! The quilt is saturated and it splashed when I dove into it! I'm so c-o-o-ld!'

"We felt sorry for her but couldn't help laughing. Dad got a towel and wrapped it around her head and shoulders."

"Your poor mom," Alex said while laughing. "It makes me shiver just thinking about it."

Leora asked, "How did the quilt get wet?"

Theodore continued, "The tent had leaked just like Mom had said, and the quilt was in the lowest part of the floor. All the water had run to that corner and the quilt soaked it up. It quit raining for a few minutes and we went outside. We saw that it wasn't just our tent that had leaked. All of the tents in the camp ground had leaked. Everywhere you looked tents had different colored table clothes, garbage bags and blankets draped over them. It looked so strange. We covered our tent with everything we could find. It started raining again so we went back inside."

"What did your dad do?"

"Dad said that it had rained so much that the water had worked through the tent fabric. After that, all it did was to filter the rain for the next couple of days. We had to keep drying the floor. We stayed mostly dry by keeping away from the wet corner. We couldn't go outside to use the camp stove so we had to go to town to buy sandwich stuff and dry our things at the laundry mat. Finally, Dad got tired of driving back and forth. He brought the stove into the tent to cook. Believe it or not, the stove dried the tent from the inside out, then it was water proof again. We were able to take the things off of our tent. We were the only nice looking tent in the park."

Alex's mom said, "I guess everyone wondered how your tent dried out and theirs didn't."

"I didn't think about that," Theodore said thoughtfully. "They probably did. Well, it finally quit raining and when the outside of our tent dried, we just packed up and left. I remember people staring at us as we folded up our tent. I guess they still had to wait for their tents to dry out." Theodore chuckled, "Maybe they thought we were better campers than they were."

"Maybe they thought that you didn't know that you had to wait for your tent to dry before you pack it up," added Dad.

Theodore chuckled again and said, "Hmm. Maybe you're right. Maybe instead of admiring us, they were thinking how dumb we were." Everyone laughed along with Theodore.

Alex said, "Let me tell you about Derick and Wally in the park." He stood up and acted out the story just as he had done at the Norton's house.

The laughter was contagious. Each story made someone think of another funny story. Alex sipped his hot chocolate and listened to his dad, mom, sister, and Theodore. The laughter, the stories, and the fire made it feel a little like Christmas.

Theodore laughed until his sides hurt and he was sure he couldn't stand any more. He noticed how happy his heart felt and thought, "This is what I've been missing. I wish it was like this at my house."

The grandfather clock chimed. Mom looked outside and said, "Hey, it isn't raining! How about pizza?" As everyone cheered, she said, "I'll call you when it's ready," and then went to the kitchen.

Dad answered the ringing phone. He handed it to Theodore and said, "It's your Aunt Betty."

Theodore took the phone and said, "Hello...We were telling stories and jokes...No, Mr. Foster said he would bring me home and Mrs. Foster is cooking pizza...Please, may I stay longer?...Okay. I'll ask him. Bye." Visibly disappointed, Theodore asked, "Mr. Foster, could you bring me home?"

"Sure," said Mr. Foster. "I'm sorry you can't stay longer and eat with us."

Alex and his family gathered around Theodore, who said, "I sure had a good time. Thanks."

"It was nice having you over," said Mrs. Foster. "Come again soon."

"I'll do my best," Theodore replied.

"Let's go," Dad said.

Mr. Foster got in the truck behind the steering wheel while Alex and Theodore were getting in from the other side.

Mrs. Foster hurried down the steps, carrying a bag. She said, "Here are your clothes, Theodore. I dried them for you. You can bring Alex's clothes back on your next visit."

Theodore said, "Thanks," as he took the bag and put it on his lap.

The truck backed out and Theodore asked Alex, "Will you be at school tomorrow?"

"Yes. After school I'm going to the doctor and, hopefully, will get rid of these bandages," Alex said with pleasure.

Theodore said, "That'll be good." They talked as Mr. Foster followed Theodore's directions as he drove across town. After several turns, Theodore pointed and said, "That's my house."

Mr. Foster parked the truck in the drive way as Mr. and Mrs. Bennett stepped out onto the porch. Theodore jumped from the truck, carrying the bag, and joined his aunt and uncle.

The Dog Was Adopted Too

Mr. Bennett called out, "Thanks."

"No problem, Samuel," Mr. Foster said. "Phone my wife and make plans to come over."

"Thanks, I will," said Mrs. Bennett. She gave Theodore a one-armed hug and waved good-bye as the truck left.

Alex said earnestly, "Dad, thanks for inviting Theodore over."

"You're welcome," Dad said. "I think the rain was God's way for you and Theodore to get to know each other better."

Mr. Foster drove the truck back home and parked in the drive way. He and Alex got out and went into the house which smelled like pizza and was very warm. Dad told Alex to open a couple of windows then went to the fireplace and moved the wood around so the fire would burn out sooner.

Mrs. Foster called out, "The pizza is on the table. Come and get it."

As Alex ate he said, between bites, "Dad invited Theodore's family to visit us."

Mrs. Foster said, "I know. Betty called and they're coming over for dinner tomorrow evening."

"Great!" said Alex and gave each parent a big hug. He said, "You're the best."

"I guess if you were able to go to the park, you're able to go to church," Dad said.

As soon as they arrived at church, Alex's friends gathered and asked him about his hand. When Theodore came into the room, Alex called him over and everyone greeted him. Theodore smiled widely as he stood with the boys. The teacher asked them to be seated.

Instead of sitting in the back of the class, Theodore sat at the same table with his friends. He looked from face to face around the room. There were still some of the boys that he hadn't met yet, but he figured that eventually he would get to know them all.

Suddenly, Theodore was aware of the significance of what had just taken place. For so long, he had wanted to have friends. He turned around and looked at the chair in the far corner where he used to sit. He was so pleased to be surrounded by his new friends.

Theodore looked up at his teacher and saw that he was smiling back at him with a sparkle in his eyes. Theodore returned a large genuine smile.

Chapter Nine
Wednesday Night
No Ordinary Boat ride

Alex's family returned home from church. The smell from the fireplace was still in the air and the happy Christmas-like feeling of the visit still hung over his family. Mom put the cushions back on the floor in a semi-circle and sat on one of them near the fireplace. She patted on another cushion and her husband and two children each sat down.

"It was so nice to sit by the fire earlier and I just wanted to continue enjoying the evening," she said.

They again shared stories, and laughed until bedtime. They stood quietly, hugged each other and said, "I love you." Each wore a pleasant smile as they walked to their bed rooms.

Alex dressed for bed then decided to read his Bible lesson. He opened the Bible to Matthew, chapter 14. He had previously read verses 22 and 23 which had told that Jesus first sent the disciples to the boat, then sent the multitudes away before going to the mountains to pray.

He began reading Matthew 14:24-33:

"But the boat was now in the middle of the sea, tossed by the waves, for the wind was contrary. Now in the fourth watch of the night Jesus went to them, walking on the sea. When the disciples saw Him

The Dog Was Adopted Too

walking on the sea, they were troubled, saying, 'It is a ghost!' and cried out for fear. But immediately Jesus spoke to them, saying, 'Be of good cheer! It is I; do not be afraid.' Peter answered Him and said, 'Lord, if it is You, command me to come to You on the water.' So He said, 'Come.' And when Peter had come down out of the boat, he walked on the water to go to Jesus. But when he saw that the wind was boisterous, he was afraid; and beginning to sink he cried out, saying, 'Lord, save me!' Immediately Jesus stretched out His hand and caught him, and said to him, 'O you of little faith, why did you doubt?' When they got into the boat, the wind ceased. Then those who were in the boat came and worshiped Him, saying, 'Truly You are the Son of God.'"

"Wow!" Alex thought. "That must have been exciting. It's strange that the disciples didn't know Jesus was God's Son until He stopped the wind."

Alex closed his papers inside the Bible and put them on the nightstand. He got up, walked down the hall, and knocked on his parent's bedroom door.

Leora heard Alex knocking on the door. She rubbed her eyes as she joined him and whispered, "What's going on?"

Dad said, "What is it?"

"I have a question about the story of Peter walking on the water," Alex said through the closed door. "Why did the disciples need to see Jesus stop the wind before they believed He was God's Son?"

"The disciples were ordinary people with regular jobs and were living with their families," Dad said. "Each man believed Jesus was the Messiah but still ..."

"What's that?" Leora asked seriously.

Dad stopped talking. He and his wife, still in the bed room, and Alex, standing at the bed room door, looked around and quietly listened. The house was silent.

Mom asked "What's what?"

"A mess – I-a," replied Leora. "You said that the disciples believed Jesus was a mess – I-a."

Relieved that there was no intruder making unexpected sounds, everyone relaxed and laughed at themselves.

"The Messiah is Jesus," answered Dad. "He is the one that the prophets told would come to save God's people."

"Oh" said Leora thoughtfully.

"Like I was saying," continued Dad. "The disciples believed Jesus was the Messiah, or the one sent by God, but they still didn't know or understand everything about Him. When Jesus called them to be disciples, He taught them about God, and Himself, as they traveled."

"The disciples," Mom added, "didn't have the New Testament. It was like their lives were writing the Bible. I think that when they saw Jesus do miracles, their understanding and faith grew."

"I'd like that!" Leora said, "It would be like being at a magic show all the time."

"So," said Alex, "the disciples were just ordinary people like you and me."

"That's right," answered Dad. "They were ordinary people who had been chosen by God to learn and spread the gospel news to the world around them."

Alex said, "I have another question. What does boisterous mean?"

Leora knocked on the door and said, "I know! I know! Boy stress is what boys worry about." Her delighted family laughed again.

Leora folded her arms, glared at Alex and asked "What's so funny?"

Dad said, "No, honey. Alex didn't say, 'boy stress.' He said, 'boisterous.' That means the wind blew strongly and made the sea have rough waves."

"Oh," Leora said softly and lowered her arms as she looked at the floor.

Alex softly patted his little sister on her back and said, "That makes sense. They were in a storm."

The grandfather clock chimed 9 o'clock. Dad said, "It's late. Go back to bed."

Alex returned to his room and glanced over the Bible scriptures again. He picked up his paper and wrote:

1. Jesus went to the mountains to pray.
2. He walked on the water.
3. The scared disciples thought Jesus was a ghost.
4. Peter asked Jesus to call him.
5. Jesus said, "Come."
6. Peter walked on water until he noticed the waves and sank.

7. Peter said, "Lord, save me."
8. Jesus reached out and caught him.
9. When they got back to the boat Jesus stopped the wind.
10. Jesus asked Peter why he doubted.
11. The disciples knew that Jesus really was the Son of God.

Alex returned the Bible and paper to the nightstand, turned off the lamp, and lay down. The rain had started again, and he could hear the wind blowing as it swayed the trees. The streetlights cast dancing tree shadows on his ceiling, giving him the creeps. He pulled the covers up to his chin and remembered how wet and cold he had been during today's rainstorm. He went to sleep thinking about the disciples in the storm and wondered how scared he would have been if he'd been with the disciples.

The lightning flashed across the sky, lighting up the raindrops as the boat rocked up and down. Alex, caught totally by surprise, hung onto a pole that was near him. He looked around in disbelief as he became aware of voices.

"Why did Jesus send us on without Him?" one voice called.

Another shouted, "Hold on."

Alex gripped the pole tighter as a wave plunged over the side of the boat, dumping gallons of water and one unfortunate fish onto the deck near Alex's feet. As he looked at the flopping fish, he saw the water slosh over his sandals.

He said, "Sandals. I don't have any sandals."

Another voice shouted, "Wave!"

The wave hit Alex and ripped him loose from the pole. He was swept to the floor and he bumped his head against the side of the boat. When he tried to get up, the wave lifted his body up and he felt himself rushing toward the ocean. There was nothing to grab onto and he would have been swept overboard, if one of the men hadn't grabbed him.

"Are you alright, Peter?" the man asked him, then shouted, "Bartholomew, help me. Peter's been hurt."

The boat rocked back-and-forth and right-to-left, causing the men to stagger as they tried to keep their balance. The noise of the wind, rain, and the waves was so loud that he could hardly hear anything else.

Alex shouted, "My name isn't Peter!"

The deck lunged and he almost fell again. He grabbed onto the side of the boat and was surprised to see his dark, hairy arms. His clothes looked like the clothing he had seen in Bible pictures. Suddenly, his hair, which was now long, caught the wind and stuck to his face. As he held onto the boat, Alex frantically pulled the strands of hair from his eyes so he could look around and make sense of his situation. He rocked with the boat as he tried to see where he was. He saw the nets, the mast, and the sails. The pole he had been holding onto was the mast of the boat. He realized he was in an ancient boat in a very violent storm.

He thought, "Well, that takes care of where I am. Now, how did I get here?"

One of the men shouted, "Andrew, There's something wrong with your brother."

"I'm coming, James." Alex looked in the direction of the voice that came from across the boat. Through the rain, Alex could see a man holding onto the side of the boat and pulling himself along as he came toward him. "Peter, are you alright?" Andrew shouted.

Alex looked at the men around him. "Andrew. James. Bartholomew," Alex said, "I'm in a boat with the disciples."

Andrew looked worried as he shouted, "Yes, Brother. Don't you remember…?" The wind blew the sound of Andrew's voice away as he pointed toward each man. Alex remembered memorizing the names of the disciples in Matthew 10.

He read Andrew's lips, "James, John, Phillip, Bartholomew, Thomas, Matthew, Thaddeus, Simon, Judas, James, you, and me."

The boat tugged at Alex's arms as he realized, "This is the story of Peter walking on the water. I'm dreaming," Alex sighed with relief.

Andrew took hold of Alex's shoulder and looked into the eyes that he believed belonged to Peter. He asked, "What?"

Someone shouted, "Look. What is that out on the water?" Andrew, Alex, and the other disciples turned and looked where the man was pointing.

The men yelled, "It's a ghost!"

"A ghost?" Alex asked himself aloud. He watched the small figure of a man walking on the water as the wind blew his hair and clothes around. Alex thought, "That's a strange place for a man to walk."

The Dog Was Adopted Too

Suddenly the most wonderful voice in the universe called to them, "Be of good cheer; it is I; be not afraid."

Alex had heard the voice clearly. It had sounded like a beautiful, heavenly orchestra. Looking beyond Thaddeus, his heart jumped for joy.

"It's Jesus!" he shouted.

Alex strained his eyes to see Jesus walking on the water and thought, "Dream or no dream, I'm going to see Jesus."

Remembering what Peter had said, he shouted, "Lord, if it is You, call me to come to You on the water."

Jesus, said, "Come."

The sound of Jesus' voice made Alex catch his breath.

The happy voice in Alex's heart and mind shouted out, "I'm coming."

Alex felt just as excited as Peter must have felt when Jesus had called him, because Alex forgot about the roaring winds, the mighty waves, the ear-shattering thunder and blinding lightening. The boat lunged and Alex steadied himself as he climbed over the side of the rocking boat. The boat rose as the bow left the water. Alex's hand felt a braided rope attached to the boat and he desperately clung to it. The boat slammed back down and almost threw Alex into the water as if trying to rid itself of the intruder. For a moment, the boat floated as if preparing for another rocking lunge. Alex quickly lowered himself down to the water. His right foot felt something solid, but Alex knew the waves were only water. He put out his other foot and felt the same solid surface. He released the rope, and to his amazement, even with all the waves, he was able to stand. A wave lifted him up and the boat surged away as if finally free. Through it all, Alex's eyes were locked on Jesus.

The wind continued to tug at his hair and clothes, but all he was aware of was Jesus walking toward him. He stepped around and over the waves until he realized that they had no effect on his balance. The nearer he got to Jesus, the faster he walked until finally he was almost running.

As he hurried along he thought to himself, "Wow, I'm walking on water." Then he asked himself, "How can I be doing this?"

He glanced down to see if he was really on water or a floor. He looked back up to Jesus who was extending His hands toward him.

Alex smiled until a wave tripped him. Another wave rushed toward him. He tried to jump over it, but fell. He reached forward with his arms and caught himself as if he were on a wet, solid floor. He struggled to his feet and saw that he was standing only a few feet from Jesus.

He stepped toward Jesus, but again glanced away each time a wave splashed against him. Without warning, he felt his feet go through the surface of the water, up to his ankles. He tried to walk, lost his balance, and fell forward. He put out his hands to catch himself as he had done before, but the water was no longer hard and he fell through and went underwater.

Water filled his mouth and his ears. Bubbles bumped his face. The sounds of the storm were muffled as he swam under the water. Each time the lightening lit the sky, he saw the shadows of Jesus' feet walking nearer to him, above the water. He felt panic as he struggled to swim.

He thought, "I've got to get to Jesus."

His heart pounded as he swam as powerfully as he could until he broke through the surface and took a deep satisfying breath. He coughed and wiped water from his eyes and his nose.

Alex heard the sound of thunder and sensed the coolness of the wind. He felt the wave sink between the other waves, carrying him downward. Still swimming, he pushed with his arms and legs to swirl himself in a circle. He couldn't believe his eyes. He felt bewildered as he spun in the other direction. He looked around and felt as if he was swimming in a bowl. He was alone.

"Jesus, where are You?" he cried out.

Suddenly, a wave lifted him and made his stomach drop as he found himself floating on a hill of water. He started to speak, but a large, white-capped wave crashed down over his head and pushed him under. The water choked him as he swam upward, toward the shadows of Jesus' feet. New energy surged within him. He quickly surfaced and coughed the choking water from his throat. He looked around and saw Jesus steadily walking toward him.

Finally, unaffected by the water, Jesus stopped and looked down at him with love and compassion in his eyes.

Alex treaded water and waited for Jesus to rescue him. His arms and legs were getting so tired and he wondered why Jesus was waiting. Then, his thoughts went to his mother who had told him that sometimes Jesus waits patiently for us to ask for His help before taking us up out of our troubles. Alex understood that his mother had been teaching him to reach and call out to Jesus. He knew he had to lift his arms up toward Jesus, but he fearfully thought that he would sink when he quit treading water.

Alex remembered what Peter had told Jesus. He collected all his courage and shouted, "Jesus, save me!"

Reaching upward, he closed his eyes and began sinking. Suddenly, strong hands grabbed him, and pulled him up. He reopened his eyes, and saw Jesus' perfect hands gripping his arms.

Jesus pulled Alex up and held him in his arms. Alex and Jesus were face-to-face. He looked in Jesus' eyes and saw love that was deeper than the love that he had seen in his parent's eyes. He felt peace within his heart as it swelled with joy. He tried to speak but felt like his heart was in his throat.

He was only able to whisper, "Thank you."

Jesus smiled, carried him back, and placed him on the deck of the boat.

The boat bucked like a horse in a rodeo. It rose and made Alex run backward passing the mast, which he grabbed and held onto tightly as he continued to watch Jesus. The winds and rain blew Jesus' hair and clothes like flags. The wind seemed to howl and fight stronger as if rebelling against Him. A wave washed over the boat and Alex lost sight of Jesus. He closed his eyes against the wind and water. He was sure that Jesus should have been washed overboard. Finally the heavy gusts of wind shifted direction, allowing him to reopen his eyes. Thankfully, Alex could see Jesus standing right where He had been before the crashing wave had hit Him.

Jesus' hair and clothes whipped wickedly in the raging wind. Jesus lifted His face to the heavens and raised His arms. The wind didn't gradually slow down. It just stopped. The boat gently bobbed in the water as Alex and the disciples stared at Jesus in amazement. Alex released the mast and was able to stand on his own. His ears felt strange. Just a second before, wind and rain had pelted his ears and he was barely able to hear anything at all. Now, he really couldn't hear anything because there was nothing to hear.

The silence was so profound that Alex woke up and found himself back in his bedroom. The shadows were still dancing on his ceiling and the room was quiet. He sat up, and turned on his lamp. He looked at his hands and felt his hair and clothes.

"I don't have long hair and I'm dry," he whispered. He smiled as he turned off the lamp and laid his head back onto the pillow, remembering the sights and sounds of being on the boat with the disciples. The feeling of Jesus' hands lifting him up from the water had been so awesome. His smile broadened as he remembered how perfect Jesus' hands had looked and how safe he had felt. As the memory of the dream played in his head, he drifted off to sleep again, hoping to return to the boat, the disciples, and Jesus. The wind blew Alex's hair as he held the wheel and steered the boat while watching the compass to make sure that he arrived at the proper harbor. The wind puffed and filled the sail to form a beautiful arch. The water glistened as it slipped past the boat. Birds, floating like kites high above him, filled the air with the sounds of their calls. The clouds looked like soft cotton balls floating in the bright blue sky. Alex smiled and inhaled deeply. The sea air was glorious.

He noticed that the calls of the birds began to change. It began sounding like a female voice. Last night he and the disciples thought that they had seen a ghost walking on the water, but it had turned out to be Jesus. He turned his head in both directions but didn't see any boats near him and he knew there had been no women onboard last night. He started to ask if anyone knew of a stow-away, but when he looked around again he realized that he was alone. Suddenly a hand grabbed his arm, and he let go of the wheel and jumped away. He heard the voice again, but this time it sounded familiar.

"Alex. Al-ex."

He felt the hand on his shoulder gently shaking him and watched as the sea, the sky, and the boat evaporated.

His mom repeated, "Alex, wake up! You have to get ready for school."

Realizing that he had been dreaming, he swung his legs over the side of his bed and stood up. He said, "I was having a terrific dream." He stretched, yawned and carefully rubbed his eyes.

"No black eyes, today," he told himself. He went to the closet to get his clothes.

"Don't forget about your doctor's appointment," Mom called. "And remember I'll pick you up, so don't ride the bus home."

Chapter Ten
Thursday Morning
The Broken Toy

Before long, he was riding the bus to school. His friends on the bus and at school were interested in his bandaged hand. Everywhere he went his friends asked questions. Several times during the day, he repeated the story of Wally's accident and his emergency room visit. He enjoyed feeling important but felt like his class work kept getting in the way of his storytelling.

The final school bell rang. He walked outside to wait for his bus and was talking with his friends until he heard a car horn. He looked around and saw his mom's van parked in the "Student pick-up" line.

He said, "How could I have forgotten my doctor's visit?" He told his friends, "I have to go." He picked up his books and sprinted to the van.

On the way to the doctor's office, Mom kept looking at her watch and searching for openings in the traffic. Finally the van drove into the doctor's parking lot. Alex and his mom hurried inside. Mom signed Alex's name on a paper and then sat next to each other.

After a few minutes, a woman called, "Alex Foster," and led them to the examination room. She took his temperature, checked his pulse and promised that the doctor would soon be with them. She left, closing the door behind her. Alex looked at the charts around the room and recognized some of the terms that he had studied in school. Just as he located a chart showing the bones in the hand, Doctor Brown knocked on the door, walked in, and greeted them.

As he removed Alex's bandages, he joked, "Don't you know to keep your hands out of a dog's mouth?"

Alex smiled at the doctor's joke. As the bandages were lifted, the cool air felt good on his hand, which looked and smelled strange. The doctor turned Alex's hand over and told him to make a fist and to wiggle his fingers. His hand was sore when he made a fist, but the doctor seemed to be satisfied. Doctor Brown lightly re-wrapped Alex's hand while instructing his mom to change the bandages every day. He told her to bring him back in one week, unless the wound looked infected.

Mom thanked Dr. Brown and his nurse as they left the room. The nurse returned and smiled as she led Alex and his mom from the room. Before leaving the building, Mom paid the bill and scheduled the next visit.

As he and his mom rode home, Alex picked at the sticky fuzz left on his hand from the bandages.

Mom parked the van in the driveway. She and Alex got out and saw Dad and Leora in the garage. Mrs. Foster led the way to show Alex's hand to Mr. Foster and Leora.

Mr. Foster smiled as he looked at his son's hand and said, "Well, that should feel a lot better."

"It does," replied Alex.

Seeing the fuzz on Alex's hand Leora asked, "Ugh! What is that stuff?"

Alex curved his fingers like claws and reached toward her and said, "That's what I saved for you."

"No-o-o-o!" she shouted, and hid behind her mom.

"Oh," said Dad, "Mr. Norton called and said you could visit Wally today."

"May I go now?" Alex asked excitedly.

"Yes, but don't stay too long," Dad replied.

"Great! Thanks," said Alex and jogged to the Norton's house leaving Leora pouting in disappointment.

Meanwhile, Theodore was visiting the Norton family and was resting in a comfortable chair in their living room. The sunlight shown through the windows and lit the room brightly. Theodore looked around at the pictures on the walls and the flowers on the coffee table. Another chair, a love seat, and a matching couch were arranged in a semicircle around the room. Mr. Norton was sitting by himself at one end of the love seat. Frances and her friend, Mrs. Pam, were sitting on either end of the couch on the other side of the room.

Visiting the Norton's home always made Theodore feel good. He and the Norton's often talked and prayed for each other, which helped them work through many of their emotional problems. Most conversations were fun like the story about Wally playing in the water. He and Frances had been at the park, watching the dog splash around in the pond. With no warning, Wally had run from the pond and had shaken himself sprinkling water all over both of them.

Today, the conversation started with Wally's accident and moved on to the loss of Theodore's parents.

He said, "When my parents died I was confused about where they were. Do you know what I mean? How were they here one minute and then gone the next? Nothing made me feel good, and I still don't know what to do most of the time." Looking at Frances, he continued, "Since I moved in with my uncle and aunt, the only friends that I had here were you and your dad and Wally, of course. Then, I met Alex last week and everything changed. Last night at church, he invited me to sit with a lot of boys in class. That was great! I'm hoping they will all become my friends."

Mrs. Pam said, "I know what you mean, Theodore. My world fell apart when my husband died, and I was very sad. I prayed and went to church, but bad things kept happening. My water well and my heater broke. A storm messed up my house, and my roof leaked. I got sick and was in the hospital a lot. I felt like God had left me until my pastor and some friends talked to me. Finally, after a while, I started to feel better, got a job and a new car, and moved to a new city. Now, I have a house with running water! God has given me new happiness, a new church, and friends. It was hard, but I've learned that God helps me."

Frances said, "Yes, I know what you mean, too. When my mom died, I felt like I had a giant hole in my heart. I still had friends but they didn't know what to say, so they didn't come around so often. I was alone a lot, too. Someone told me a story that helped me. It was called 'The Broken Toy Story.'* Would you like to hear it? It could help you, too."

"Sure," Theodore said.

"A little girl," Frances began, "had a beautiful doll that was her favorite toy. One day something happened, and the doll was broken. All she thought about was the doll, and she was always sad. Someone took her to a doll repair shop, and she handed the doll to the repairman. He looked at it and gathered his tools, but before he could start his work, the little girl began crying. She snatched the doll back and hugged it close to her. Patiently, the man persuaded her to give it back to him, but again she took it away before he could fix it. All of her attention was focused on the doll.

"Someone explained to her that the only way for the doll to be fixed was for her to trust the man and leave it with him. Finally, she let him keep her doll and before long, she had it back, good as new."

Frances said, "When I heard that story, it told me how much God wanted to help me with my problem, which was a broken heart. I tried to fix it myself. I didn't pray and ask God to help me, because I hadn't learned to trust Him yet. Theodore, you have to trust God. I finally did, and now I'm a lot better."

Theodore said, "That's why I've wanted to have friends. I'm tired of being sad all the time."

Frances said, "You have to do like the little girl did. She finally focused on God, and let Him fix her problems. You have to let Him be the 'fixer' of your heart, and then you'll start getting better. It's hard to do, but it gets easier. Pray and read the Bible."

"But, Frances, I have been reading my Bible and praying," Theodore said, "but I still feel sad. I'm always thinking about Mom, Dad and Ronnie. I miss them all the time!"

"Theodore," Frances said softly, "May I ask you a personal question?"

"Sure, I guess so," answered Theodore.

Frances looked seriously into Theodore's eyes, "What happened the day that your parents died?"

"Oh!" responded Theodore.

"You don't have to answer if you don't want to. It's just that you haven't told us much about it. I thought that it might help if you did," said Frances in a tender voice.

"No, I don't mind. It's just that since the day that my parents died, no one but the police, a lawyer and a judge have asked me about it. I was surprised. It makes me feel good that you want to know."

Theodore looked at each person in the room then he closed his eyes and took a deep breath. He looked back up at Frances and said, "My mom and dad went to a retirement party. Ronnie and I didn't want to go, because it didn't sound like much fun. They were planning to be back at 4:00 to take Ronnie and me to the movies."

"At 10 o'clock that morning, mom kissed and hugged me for an especially long time before getting into the car with Dad. I used to wonder if she knew that she wouldn't see me again. I finally decided that if she had known what was going to happen she wouldn't have left us at all."

Theodore stopped and silently looked out the window. After a couple of minutes, he said, "I miss Mom's hugs. I always knew that she loved me and she made me feel so safe. She always had the nicest perfume."

Theodore looked around the room and saw Frances and Mrs. Pam wiping their eyes. He continued, "After our parents left, Ronnie and I played games, read and talked all day. After eating lunch, we started to get bored so we decided to watch a movie. I don't remember which one it was though. Just as the movie ended the phone rang. It was Dad. He said that he and Mom would be back in half an hour. He told us to get cleaned up for the movies."

"We jumped up and got ready to go and watched TV while we waited. A long time went by, so we went outside to wait. We called Mom and Dad's cell phones, but no one answered. Ronnie and I were really worried. We went back inside and I called one of our cousins, Sherry. She and her husband said that they would come over to wait with us. After a few minutes, we heard two car doors close.

"Ronnie said, 'That was quick.' He ran and opened the door then just stood there. He said, 'Theodore come here, hurry!' His voice sounded so strange that I hurried to the door. We watched as a policeman and a policewoman walked to our front door.

"The tall policeman looked down at us and asked, 'Does Mr. and Mrs. Moore live here?'

"Ronnie said, 'Yes but they aren't here right now.'

"The policewoman asked if anyone was with us. I told her that our cousin, Sherry, would be here soon.

"The policeman asked if he and the lady police officer could come in and wait with us. We let them in, and I asked if anything was wrong. The policewoman said that we would have to wait until Sherry got there.

"Ronnie and I were scared, so we just sat next to each other without talking. After a while, we heard another car. Ronnie and I ran to the door and let Sherry and George in. Sherry was crying and asked, 'Why are the police here? Is everything alright?' When she saw the police on our couch she almost fell and her husband, George, grabbed her.

"The policewoman asked us to take her to the kitchen so she could have some water. Just as I gave her the glass of water, Sherry screamed. Ronnie and I hurried to the living room. We saw George hugging Sherry who was crying.

"Ronnie ran and hugged Sherry. He asked, 'What's wrong, Sherry? George, what happened?' All that I could hear was my heart beating in my ears." Theodore sniffed and wiped at his eyes.

He finally said, "I don't remember much about what was said, but when everything quieted down, Ronnie and I found out that we didn't have parents anymore."

Theodore sat and stared blankly out of the window and said, "Nobody knew why, but there was a head-on collision. The man who hit my mom and dad died too.

"Sherry and George and both sets of our aunts and uncles stayed for a few days. After the funeral, some people came over and looked at the papers that mom and dad had written. They said that we would be taken to a foster home while somebody decided who we would live with. Ronnie and I cried when we were put in the car and taken away. Our family waved bye to us and cried as we drove off. We stayed with a nice family for a little while until we were sent to our new families."

Frances spoke with sadness in her voice and said, "I'm sorry. That is so sad."

"Yes." Theodore said, "I want to be with Ronnie and my parents so much. Sometimes I am so sad that I feel like I might just explode. I want to know where my mom and dad are. I can't help it, Frances. I want to be with them."

Frances blotted her eyes and cleared her throat and asked, "Were your parents Christians?"

"Sure," replied Theodore, "Mom and Dad took us to church all the time."

The Dog Was Adopted Too

"Then, I know where your parents are," Frances said.

Theodore sat up straight and looked at her with new interest.

Frances continued, "Your mom and dad are where all Christians go when they die. They are with God and are being protected by Him just like my mom."

Theodore looked at Frances with hurt in his eyes and said in a low, sad voice, "I want things to be like they used to be. I want to be home with Mom, Dad, and Ronnie." Theodore stood up and walked to the window. He looked outside without really seeing anything.

Frances said, "I know how you feel, but things are different now and we can't go back. We have to trust God to help us." She rose and joined Theodore at the window. She watched the wind gently sway the tree branches. Without looking at Theodore, she said quietly, "I miss my mom, too. I believe that God let us become friends so we can comfort each other."

Theodore was quiet. A piece of paper caught his attention as it hopped and then slid across the yard. He said, "I used to have bad dreams almost every night before Ronnie and I moved in with our new families."

Frances asked, "Do you still have those dreams?"

"No," answered Theodore.

"So, you did get better," Frances said with a slight smile.

Theodore said, "Not too much at first. When I started going to school here, I sometimes forgot about being sad. I guess I do feel a little better."

Frances asked, "Do you think that it's God who helped you to feel better?"

"I guess," Theodore said.

"You have to believe that God loves and cares for you," advised Frances.

Theodore said. "I know. I'm trying." He watched the leaves swaying and thought of his mom. He glanced at Frances then pointed to the trees. He said, "I just remembered something that my mom told me. She said that God is like the wind. You can't see the wind, but you can see the trees that are moved by the wind. That proves the wind is there. She said something like, you can't see God, but if you watch you can see Him by the good things that you get. I think she said blessings or some other Bible word."

Frances turned away from the window and said, "What a wonderful memory. I think that God made you think of that right now for a reason. It's what we've been talking about. You can see God moving in your life by the way that you are feeling better and by getting new friends. That's how you can know that God is real and that He loves you."

Theodore smiled and said, "Sure! That's what she meant. I didn't understand it back then, but you're right." He smiled wider and said, "My mom sure was smart."

"I'm glad you remember things like that," Frances said.

Mr. Norton said, "You're mom must have been very wise."

Theodore said, "I can't wait to call Ronnie to see if he remembers that too."

"Do you get to see Ronnie very often?" asked Mrs. Pam from across the room.

Theodore walked back and stood next to his chair. He looked at Mrs. Pam and thought that she always dressed nice and smelled so good. He smiled and answered, "Not since I moved here, but we talk on the phone. He misses me too. We wish we could visit each other."

"Have you told your family that you want to see him?" asked Frances.

"I did at first, and Ronnie asked his family too. We kept being told that we live too far apart, so we finally quit asking," Theodore said sadly.

"You should ask again. I think that visiting Ronnie would make you feel better."

"It would help both of us," he said.

"You need to talk to your aunt and uncle about it again," advised Frances.

"I know." He looked at the clock on the wall and said, "I'd better go."

He and Frances walked to the door. Theodore waved bye to everyone and turned to leave. Just as Frances touched the doorknob, the doorbell rang.

Chapter Eleven
Thursday Evening
He's The One

Frances opened the door and said, "Alex! Come in."

Alex stepped inside and said, "Hi."

"I'm so sorry that Wally bit you," Frances said sincerely. "How is your hand?"

"It's okay," Alex replied. As Frances was closing the door, he saw Theodore and said with surprise, "Hey! I didn't know that you knew each other!"

Theodore said, "Yeah, and I didn't know that it was Wally that had bit you." He looked at Alex's lightly bandaged hand and said, "That looks better."

Alex said, "Yea, it feels a lot better, too." He turned to Frances and said, "Mr. Norton called and said that I could see Wally today. May I?"

Frances said, "Sure, but first, let me introduce you to my friend, Mrs. Pam."

Alex looked across the room, and saw a pretty lady sitting in a chair. He smiled, and said, "Hi."

Mrs. Pam said, "Very nice to meet you."

"This is the young man who offers to help me," said Mr. Norton.

"That's very nice of you," Mrs. Pam commented.

"Thanks," said Alex.

Mr. Norton said, "Come here and let me see your hand, Alex."

Alex walked over to Mr. Norton who took his bandaged hand and looked at both sides. He lightly patted Alex's hand and said, "I'm so sorry that Wally bit you. You, of all people, didn't deserve that."

Alex felt so bad when he saw how regretful Mr. Norton was. Alex said, "I'm okay. I'm just hoping that Wally gets better soon."

Frances said, "Come with me." She led the boys across the room and opened the door. Wally lay on his doggie bed with cloth bandages wrapped around his ribs. He raised his head, looked at the boys and made a slap, slap, slap noise as he wagged his tail against the bed. Frances said, "We have to keep the door closed because Dr. Marks said he needs to be kept quiet for a while."

Theodore and Alex petted Wally while trying to keep him from getting up. Wally licked both boys and wiggled and squirmed but obediently stayed on his bed. The boys laughed as they decided that Wally was a "jolly collie."

"When did you get Wally?" Theodore asked Frances.

"It was a long time before my mom died. My parents had a friend named Mr. Keith who had bought Wally from a collie farm. We visited Mr. Keith a lot, so I got to know and love Wally. Well, Mr. Keith had him for about a year when, for some reason, he had to move. The place that he moved to wouldn't allow dogs, so he had to find a new home for him. He asked if I would like to have Wally. I told him that I sure would, and my parents agreed."

Theodore hugged Wally lightly around the neck and said, "So, your dog was adopted, too." He looked at Frances and asked, "You wanted him before you adopted him?"

"Well, I never thought about it that way. I guess I did adopt him and yes, I loved him. I still love him, and I'm happy that I have him. He was very good company for me when my mom died."

Alex said, "Wally is lucky to be adopted by a family who loves him so much."

"He sure is," said Frances.

Theodore stood up and said, "I need to go home."

"I'll see you at my house in a little while," Alex said.

Theodore said, "Okay," and he and Frances left the room. Alex thought he saw Theodore wipe his eyes on his sleeve as he disappeared through the door.

Soon, Frances returned to Alex and Wally. Both boy and dog were having a secret conversation.

Frances said, "I can't believe this! Remember the boy that I said needed friends? He's the one!"

"What a coincidence," Alex commented.

"I don't think it's a coincidence. I think God wanted him to have you for a friend. I just can't believe that he's going to your house tonight!" Frances said in amazement.

Alex told her about the rainstorm and Theodore's unexpected visit. "We took him home and our parents planned a dinner for tonight. My dad agrees with you. He said that he thought God arranged the rain so we could become friends."

"I'm constantly amazed about the things that God does," Frances said.

"Frances, what do I talk to Theodore about at dinner tonight?" asked Alex.

"You didn't look like you had a problem talking to him while he was here," stated Frances.

"Yeah, but we were talking about Wally," replied Alex.

"Well then, that must be the secret. Talk about something you have in common," reasoned Frances.

"I guess so," Alex said, and then asked, "Was Theodore crying when he left?"

"I didn't see him crying. Why do you ask?" asked Frances.

"I thought I saw him wipe his eyes on his shirt sleeve," said Alex. "It just looked like he was wiping tears."

"Maybe he was crying. He had been talking about his family before you got here. Ask him about it when he gets to your house." Frances looked worried then said, "Wally needs to rest. Let's go to the living room."

"Be a good boy," Alex said as he patted the dog once again. He joined Frances, who closed the door as the two friends left the room.

"I have to go do my homework. Theodore and his family will be at my house soon," Alex said as he walked to the front door and stopped. He turned back to Frances and said, "Thanks for letting me see Wally. You know he didn't mean to bite me."

"I didn't think he did. He's a good dog," Frances said as she opened the door.

"He sure is. I'll see you later," said Alex as he walked down the steps.

Frances waved and said, "Let me know if Theodore is alright."

Alex waved back and said, "I will."

Alex hurried home and Mom said, "You'd better go do your homework. The Bennett's will be here in a little while, as soon as Theodore is through with his homework." Alex got his books and in less time than usual was finished.

When he left his room, his nose led him to the kitchen where his mom was stirring a pot. She turned around, almost bumping into him. "Oh, Alex!" she said, "You startled me." She pointed to a bowl of potato salad and said, "Put plastic wrap on the salad and take it outside to the picnic table."

Alex covered the bowl and took it outside. He put the bowl down and noticed that the picnic table had been set for seven people. He walked back into the house just in time to see his parents inviting Theodore, his aunt, and his uncle inside. Each was carrying a container of food.

"Let's put these things on the table outside," said Mom. Alex took the plate of cookies from Mrs. Betty and led the way through the house and outside to the patio. As they passed through the kitchen, Alex's mom took a pitcher of lemonade from the refrigerator and a bowl of ice from the freezer.

Alex put the cookies down and Theodore handed him a bag. He told Alex, "Don't eat this. It's your clothes that I wore home yesterday."

Alex chuckled, "Thanks for the warning," he said as he put the bag under his chair.

When everyone was seated, Dad said the blessing. Alex was pleased about how easily the conversations went. He decided that he had been worrying about nothing.

After the meal, the adults and Leora, who was munching on cookies, went to the patio chairs. Alex and Theodore walked to the swing across the yard and drank lemonade as they talked.

Swinging slowly, Theodore asked, "Are you still in trouble with your dad about the accident at church?"

"No," Alex answered. "He grounded me until I finished a book that he told me to read. I finished it Monday afternoon and everything is okay."

The Dog Was Adopted Too

"Are you mad at him?" Theodore asked.

"No. I was running inside the building and caused the accident. I apologized to Dad, Mom, and the girls. No one is mad at me now."

Alex looked down at his glass then cleared his throat nervously. "Theodore," he began, "I need to ask you a question."

Theodore, sensing the change in Alex's mood, said, "Sure, is something wrong?"

"It's about you and Wally."

"Oh, Wally is a terrific dog! When I first moved here, I liked to walk around town until I discovered the park. I used to wander around the pond and watch the ducks. Sometimes I even saw you and the other guys playing with Wally. One day when no one else was around, Wally came to me and we played fetch, and chased each other. Best of all, we would sit in the shade in the edge of the woods or near the pond. I talked and Wally listened to me. A lot of times he wagged his tail and bounced around and made me forget my troubles."

Theodore looked up at the dark sky. He cleared his throat, looked down at his hands and continued, "Once, when I was having a really bad day, I felt like crying. Wally knew something was wrong. He stood up and just looked at me with his head cocked to the side and his eyes looking so sad. He whined, then laid down really close to me, and put his head and front feet on my lap. It felt like he was hugging me. That's the day that he became my best friend." Theodore looked away and wiped his eyes. He turned back to Alex and said, "Later, I met Frances when she was searching for him. She, and her dad, both became my friends. I've had a lot of good times talking with them at the park and their house."

"My dad told me that he had to move a lot when he was a kid." Alex said. "He told me about how hard it was trying to make new friends in a new town."

"He's right," Theodore said as he sighed and leaned back against the swing. He looked at Alex and said, "I grew up having friends just like you do. I even had a dog named Bouncer."

"Bouncer?" Alex asked. "Why did you call him that?"

"Well, think about Wally," Theodore replied. "Bouncer did just like Wally does. He bounced all the time."

"I can see that happening," Alex said as he looked thoughtfully. "I wonder what is behind Wally's name."

"Maybe he wallowed in different things when he was a puppy," Theodore reasoned.

Alex and Theodore named all the dirty, stinky things that a dog could wallow in. They laughed so loudly that their parents and Leora looked at them and laughed, too.

Theodore finally stopped laughing, took a deep breath and blew it out loudly. He said, "Man oh man! Anyway, Fred, Carl, Rick and I used to ride bikes and play together. We would sleep over at each other's houses, and go to each other's birthday parties. One night after church, Carl and I were sitting in the back pew of the auditorium waiting for our parents to finish choir practice."

"I know what that's like," laughed Alex.

Theodore chuckled and continued, "We lay down and talked. I guess the music was really soothing because we fell asleep."

"Oh, man!" Alex groaned.

Theodore said, "I don't know how long we had slept, but when I woke up I heard my mom crying and Carl's mom was saying something about calling the police."

"What happened?" Alex asked with excitement in his voice.

"I didn't know," replied Theodore. "I sat up to see what was going on. They were sitting near the front of the church all alone. I reached over and woke Carl up. I whispered and told him that something was wrong. We listened for a little bit, but their voices got so low that we couldn't hear them anymore. We eased up the aisle so we could hear them better. Mom and Mrs. Graham were praying so Carl and I quietly sat down next to them until they finished.

"When Mom said, 'Amen,' I asked her what had happened. She turned and saw me and squealed. She hugged me so tight that I could hardly breathe. When Mrs. Graham saw Carl she hugged him and thanked Jesus."

Alex half laughed, "No way! Your folks thought that you guys were lost?"

"They sure did." laughed Theodore. "All of a sudden the church was full of choir members praising God. The police showed up and then went away. I guess we scared everyone. Some ladies even started a new Wednesday night children's class that was during choir practice time."

Theodore sat up and said, "Boy! We had a lot of good times. I'll have to tell you and the guys some of the other things that we did." Theodore sighed and said softly, "I guess that's why I've been so lonely, I miss everyone so much. I still get sad sometimes. Right now I feel a lot better."

Alex rubbed his chin, and said, "That's good." He looked at Theodore with a crooked smile and said, "Well, that's sort of what I was going to ask you about."

Theodore stopped the swing and turned and looked at Alex. He asked, "What do you want to know?"

Alex looked seriously and asked, "When you and I were visiting Wally and talking to Frances, were you cry...? Uh... I mean... did you...?" Alex sat his glass down on the swing and looking back at Theodore he tried again. "When we were with Wally... well, were you sad?"

"Oh," said Theodore as he looked toward the adults then back at Alex. "I guess I was, just for a little while."

"Did Frances or I say something that hurt your feelings?"

"No."

"What was wrong, then?" asked Alex.

There was worry in Theodore's eyes as he looked to his left and then to the right.

Chapter Twelve
Thursday Evening
The Tickets!

 Alex's question had caught Theodore by surprise. His thoughts were running in wild circles like a hamster on an exercise wheel. He had gotten emotional earlier at Frances' house when he had been talking about his parent's accident. He had wanted to leave but, when Alex arrived, Frances had invited him to go see Wally again. Petting Wally had helped him to regain his composure until Frances told how she had loved Wally before she had adopted him. The thought of being unloved came back to him and he left the room. Evidently he hadn't left soon enough. "Oh man," he whispered.

 Theodore decided that it was too late to deny his emotions. He relaxed and slumped back in the swing. He didn't feel like talking now, but Alex had asked. Alex had been such a good friend and he didn't want to hurt his feelings by refusing to answer his question. He trusted Alex and decided to be honest with him.

 Alex asked, "Theodore, are you alright. I didn't mean to upset you."

 Theodore brushed imaginary dust from the swing and looked down at the ground. He said, "You didn't say anything wrong. I just hate crying so much." He sighed and looked back up at Alex. "Yes, I was starting to cry." He sighed again then asked, "Do you remember when I said that Wally was adopted too?"

"Yeah," Alex replied, softly.

"It's just that when Frances said she already loved Wally before she got him, I thought about what a lucky dog he was to be loved first, before he was adopted." He nodded in the direction of his aunt and uncle and said, "I was just dropped into their laps when my parents died." Theodore sniffed and looked away. "They never had a chance to love me before they got me." Theodore stood up and walked a few steps away.

Alex, feeling uncomfortable, noticed that both of their lemonade glasses were empty and said, "Come with me to get more lemonade."

"You go ahead," answered Theodore. "I'll just wait here."

Alex said, "Alright." He was glad to be away from Theodore for a few minutes. He had never seen him so upset and didn't know what to say to him. Alex walked to the picnic table but saw that it had been cleared. He went to the adults who were still talking. Not wanting to interrupt their conversation, he stood quietly, waiting to be noticed.

Mrs. Bennett was saying, "Ronnie is Theodore's younger brother. When Christine and Raymond died, we were allowed only to have Theodore to live with us."

Mrs. Foster asked, "Where is Ronnie?"

Mrs. Bennett said, "Wait, I'm getting ahead of myself. I need to fill in some facts. Samuel and I were part of a three family group and we were also very close friends. Theodore is my nephew because his mother, Christine, was my sister. Theodore's family was the first group. Christine's husband, Raymond, had a brother named Ralph Moore. He and his wife, Barbara, were the second family group and Samuel and I were the third. When Theodore and Ronnie were still very young, our three families all lived in the same town. We were a close, happy family and we all loved the boys dearly. One evening Christine invited all of us to their house. During dinner, totally out-of-the-blue, Christine and Raymond said that if both of them died, they wanted one couple to raise their children. We were all surprised, but of course, we all agreed. Christine took a family photo and we even signed papers to make everything legal.

During the following years, we all moved to different parts of the country. We kept in touch by phone and wrote letters, but were never able to see each other. When the accident happened, we went to the funeral and expected to bring the children home right away. The authorities wouldn't let us take the boys because the agency had to check us out first. Our two families were sent home and the boys were placed into a foster home. Some people were sent to visit each of our families. Finally, we were told that neither of our homes was large enough to raise both boys. The decision was finally made and each of us was given one boy. It isn't what any of us wanted, but it's all we were allowed to do. We adopted Theodore and have loved him very much. We've been trying to make him happy." Mrs. Bennett stopped talking when she noticed Alex standing next to his mom.

Mom turned to Alex and asked, "What do you need, son?"

Alex asked, "May we have more lemonade and cookies?"

"The cookies are gone, but there's some lemonade in the refrigerator," Mom replied.

Alex went inside the house then returned to Theodore, carrying two glasses of lemonade.

Theodore, who had returned to the swing, took one glass and said, "I was thinking about the bowling passes that I've won. If they're still good I'd like to share them with you and the other guys all at one time. I might have enough for us to go again."

"Hey, that's a great idea!" Alex said, "I'm sure the passes are good because Mr. Walker owns the bowling alley. Let's call him." The hopeful boys trotted inside. Alex phoned Mr. Walker and told him that Theodore wanted to share the tickets with some of the guys so all of them could go bowling.

Mr. Walker almost shouted, "Alex, that's great! Sure the tickets are still good." Then he added, "When do you want to bowl?"

"We're hoping that tomorrow evening or maybe Saturday morning," Alex said.

Mr. Walker said, "Well, let me know so I can keep a couple of lanes open."

"Sure," said Alex. "I'll call you back as soon as I can. Bye."

Alex and Theodore asked their parents about the bowling plan and the idea was a hit! The boys ran back to the phone and began calling friends from Sunday school.

A half hour later, Alex told Mr. Walker goodbye, hung up the phone, and excitedly told Theodore, "It's all settled! You, Michael,

Derick, Joshua, Kevin and I are going to bowl at 10:00 on Saturday morning!"

Theodore cheered. He and Alex jumped and gave each other a really high five. After telling their parents the planned time, they ran back to the swing and happily talked about bowling, school, and church.

Theodore said, "You know, the reason that I won those passes is because I didn't have any friends. I read most of the time and I was able to find a lot of answers."

"I wondered how you won each week," Alex responded. He remembered thinking that Theodore's parents had given him the answers. He told himself, "Boy! Was I ever wrong?"

Theodore said, "At first I wanted to bowl each week, but I knew my aunt and uncle wouldn't want to be bothered by taking me. That's why I still have all of the passes."

"You talk like you don't think your aunt and uncle care about you," Alex commented.

"I'm just a bother and I'm in their way," Theodore said as he looked down.

"According to what I just heard, you're wrong about that," Alex stated.

Theodore looked up and asked, "What are you talking about?"

"When I went to get the lemonade," Alex said, "I overheard your aunt saying that she and your uncle had agreed with your parents to raise you if your parents died. She told my mom that they have always loved you and have been trying to make you happy."

Theodore looked at Alex as if he hadn't understood a single word.

Alex started to speak, but Mr. Bennett called, "Theodore, it's getting late. We have to be going."

Theodore spoke softly to Alex and confessed, "I don't know what to say."

"Just talk to them about it," suggested Alex.

Theodore said, "When I was at Frances' house, she told me to do the same thing."

"Good. Do it," encouraged Alex.

"I'm sort of nervous about it," Theodore replied. "I've always tried to avoid talking to them."

"My dad told me a long time ago that when you pray first, God gives you courage," advised Alex.

Theodore said, "Okay. Thanks."

The boys walked slowly to the front door and joined Leora and the adults who were promising to get together again. Alex and Theodore walked to the car and made plans to meet near the water fountain at school the next day.

The Bennett family drove off and the Foster family went back inside. Dad closed the door and Mom reached out and gave her son a big hug and said, "Betty told me that Theodore seems to be happier."

Dad patted Alex on the back and said, "You're doing a good thing, Son."

Alex smiled at his dad and said, "Thanks."

An hour later, after showers and prayers, all the lights in the Foster house had been turned off except for the lamp on Alex's night stand. He knew that Leora was asleep in her bedroom and he could hear his parents' voices coming from their room. He lay in his bed and thought about how well his day had turned out.

He remembered how upset he used to feel toward Theodore. He felt bad about not liking him just because he'd been winning all of the contests. He thought to himself, "How could I have been so mixed up that I couldn't see what was most important?" Now he wished that it had been his own idea to get to know him.

He wondered why Theodore had seemed so surprised when he heard that his aunt and uncle loved him. Alex decided to talk to him later at school or at church.

Alex felt good about his and Theodore's new friendship. He prayed, "Thank you God for helping me to be Theodore's friend. And God, help me to want new friends without having to be told by others. Amen."

He felt joy form in his heart and smiled. He began to feel sleepiness pull on his heavy eye lids. With his eyes half closed, he reached for his night stand and turned out his light. He lay back on his pillow, pulled his cover up to his chin and drifted off to sleep.

Chapter Thirteen
Friday Afternoon
Favorite Story

Fireworks! Rainbows! Puppies! Shooting stars! Ice cream! No words that Theodore thought of could compare with how good he felt. The school bus stopped at his house and he bounded down the steps and ran inside shouting, "Aunt Betty!" He followed the sound of her voice to the laundry room and excitedly gave her a huge hug.

"My goodness, you're in a good mood," Aunt Betty said. She kissed his cheek and said, "Come to the kitchen and eat a snack. Tell me what has brought you such joy."

Theodore mounted the snack bar stool, took a big bite of his peanut butter and jelly sandwich then washed it down with a half glass of milk. He took a deep breath and said, "Aunt Betty, I've had the best day of my life. When I got to school, I met with my friends and we planned the bowling game for tomorrow. Oh," he bit the sandwich and continued as he chewed, "Kevin wasn't at school. Did you know he's home schooled? Alex said that he works just as hard on his school work as we do."

He thirstily took another gulp of milk and said, "All day long, I saw Alex, Michael, Joshua, and Derick. We talked at lunch and recess and even when we were leaving to go home. I got on the school bus," he interrupted himself with another bite of his sandwich, swallowed and continued, "and they all waved bye to me. It's so much fun having friends at school again." He took two more bites and finished his milk.

Aunt Betty refilled his glass as he continued, "Can you and Uncle Samuel stay and watch me bowl tomorrow? All the other families are staying and I'd like you to come, too." He finished his sandwich, drank half of the milk, took a deep breath, and emptied the glass. He asked, "May I visit Frances and Wally?"

Aunt Betty laughed and hugged her nephew. "Yes, but be back before dark so you can do your homework."

"I will. Thanks." He hopped down from the stool, ran outside and hurried to the Norton's house.

Aunt Betty watched him, noticing that he had a new spring in his step. Her heart was full of joy. She felt like Theodore had just welcomed her into his life!

Uncle Samuel, who had returned home from work early, found his teary-eyed wife watching Theodore trot down the sidewalk. He asked worriedly, "What's wrong?"

"Samuel, I think he's beginning to think of us as his family. He told me that he wanted us to watch him bowl with the other families!"

Samuel hugged her and shouted, "Praise, God! Our prayers are being answered!"

"So, do you want to watch him bowl tomorrow?" asked Betty excitedly.

"I sure do!" he said. "That boy will never know how much I love him and how happy he makes me. I couldn't love him more if he had been my natural born son."

"I'm going to call Rebecca," said Betty as she reached for the phone.

"Good," said Samuel, "After all, it's her son who's helping Theodore."

Betty made the call and both women rejoiced for Theodore's happiness.

Rebecca said, "We're planning to watch Alex bowl tomorrow. Come join us."

"That sounds great!" Betty said. "We'll see you in the morning at ten."

When Mr. Norton saw Theodore approaching, he opened the back door and called, "Frances, you and Wally have another visitor."

Theodore trotted down the backdoor steps and followed the paved stones toward the outdoor furniture under the shadow of a large shade tree. Frances, Mrs. Pam, and Alex were sitting in chairs placed around the table. Frances pulled out an empty chair for Theodore. Wally, who was lying near Frances' feet, raised his head and wagged his tail as Theodore approached.

"He looks almost well, doesn't he?" asked Alex.

Theodore squatted down and scratched Wally behind his ears before he sat in the chair. He said, "Yeah. He's looks better without the bandages." Looking at Alex, he asked, "Did you tell them about tomorrow?"

"Not yet," Alex said, "I got here just before you did."

"What's going on tomorrow?" asked Frances.

Theodore sat in a chair, and both boys excitedly took turns telling about the planned bowling trip.

"That's great," said Mrs. Pam.

"It sounds like a lot of fun," responded Frances. She saw Wally turn on his side and let out a raspy doggy sigh. She said, "Wally's looking tired. Let's take him back inside and we'll get some tea."

A few minutes later, Wally was back in his room and the group of friends was sitting in the living room, sipping iced tea. Alex said, "Frances, I came over to ask you a question about a dream that I had."

Frances asked, "What was it about?"

Alex said, "I dreamed about Peter walking on the water."

"That's my favorite Bible story," Frances said.

"Why?" Alex asked.

"After my mom died, I was sad most of the time. One day I watched a TV movie about Peter walking on the water. It helped me to see myself differently and I began to be happier."

Theodore asked seriously, "How did a movie do that?"

"Well," Frances began, "the movie showed Peter doing fine walking on the water until he noticed the waves. When he quit looking at Jesus, he began to sink. It seemed like he was going to drown until he asked Jesus to save him, which Jesus did. I imagined myself being like Peter, but drowning in my sadness instead of water. I knew something special was happening in my heart, but I didn't know what to do, so I called my pastor. He told me that Jesus could have saved Peter right away, but He waited for Peter to realize that he couldn't save himself. Finally, Peter stopped struggling, reached up for Jesus and cried out, 'Save me!' That's when Jesus rescued him.

"My pastor said that Jesus was waiting for me to do the same thing. I quit trying to 'fix' myself, and asked Jesus to save me, which He did. I'm happier now, but I didn't change all at once. I had to learn to depend on Jesus little-by-little. He always helps me...when I let Him."

Alex said, "Mom told me that we have to do everything the way that Jesus has planned."

"That's right," agreed Frances. "As the old song says, 'Jesus Never Fails.'"

Theodore asked, "You told me that you still miss your mom."

"Of course I do. I think of her every day," Frances answered.

"Will I ever stop being so sad about my family?" Theodore asked emotionally.

"I've had more time to get better than you have," Frances replied, "Everybody gets better at their own pace. You'll always love your parents. I believe that God is using your new friends to help you to be happier. Just let Jesus help you with your grief."

"I'm trying so hard," Theodore said.

Mr. Norton said, "My wife was my best friend, my helper, my cook and my bookkeeper, all wrapped up in one person. When she was gone, I didn't know what to do or how to care for Frances by myself. I prayed and God sent family and friends to us. Frances is right," he said. "I found that Jesus has always been with me and has lifted me out of my grief. I still miss my darling wife, and my life is different without her, but God helps me to be happy every day."

Theodore looked at Mr. Norton and said, "God helped you and Frances to be happy." Then he looked at Mrs. Pam and said, "You told me how God helped you when your husband died and your house got torn up in a storm. You said that God has given you a new happiness."

Finally he looked at Frances and said, "You've shown me that God took care of you. I know He is taking care of me and that's why I'm starting to feel happier."

Frances smiled and said, "I'm so glad to hear you say that. Just keep watching what God does for you and don't forget to thank Him for everything."

"You are important to God," Mr. Norton said. "He loves you. God provided you with a loving family who wants you to be happy. He's been taking care of you through the loss of your parents and will continue to take care of you throughout the rest of your life."

The Dog Was Adopted Too

Theodore sat wide-eyed as he looked at the floor. He felt a strange feeling that made him lonely. He said, "I think I need to talk to my aunt and uncle." He stood up and Mr. Norton walked him to the door. He put his hand on Theodore's shoulder and whispered a short prayer. Theodore wiped his eyes on his shirtsleeve and quietly told everyone good-bye. He opened the side gate and closing it behind him, he headed home.

"God has been at work in this house," Mr. Norton said as he closed the door.

Alex started missing his parents and felt a strong urge to be with them. He told Frances, "Listening to you explain the movie has helped me understand my dream. I think that I'm supposed to focus on Jesus. He will keep me from sinking into sin or other problems. And if I do sink, He will pull me up when I call on Him."

"That's it. I'm glad I could help," said Frances.

"I have to go home," he said to Frances as he waved goodbye to Mr. Norton and Ms. Pam. Frances walked Alex to the door and everyone said their goodbyes. Alex trotted home anxious to see his family.

Frances closed the door and said, "I feel so good. God has blessed me again."

Mr. Norton rose from his chair and walked over to Frances. He put his arm around his daughter and said, "I feel it too, honey."

Mrs. Pam said, "Theodore needs our prayers. I'm so glad I was here today." She noticed the time and said, "Thanks for a lovely evening. I have to be going, too."

Frances walked Mrs. Pam to her car and returned inside. She listened to her dad humming a tune that he used to sing with her mom. Soon, Frances was humming the same tune.

Love grew in each home that evening, as each family enjoyed talking together before going to bed.

Mrs. Pam phoned some of her family and told of her time at the Norton's home. She asked them to pray for Theodore. Soon she went to bed and contentedly fell asleep.

Alex did his homework, then spent time eating and talking with his family. At bed time they all prayed for Theodore. Alex studied the Bible, then went to bed thanking God that he had become friends with Theodore.

Theodore arrived home and Aunt Betty gave him a hug which he returned. He did his homework, then talked with his aunt and uncle for a while. He really enjoyed spending time with them. They ate supper and then went to bed. He remembered to say his prayers and thanked God for his friends. He asked God to help him to continue to be happy.

As he lay in bed, he thought about the fun he would have at the bowling alley. As he drifted off to sleep, he dreamed about bowling. He made a strike every time he threw the ball. He rolled the ball down the street and made a strike with street lights instead of bowling pins. He threw the ball into a tree and "Strike," apples hit the ground. He was suddenly in the park and tossed the ball across the pond and hit ducks. Duck eggs flew everywhere, turned into blue ribbons, and floated down to the water. He chuckled in his sleep as fish turned into bowling pins and he began bowling under water.

God smiled down on His sleeping children. His grace was helping each life grow in His love and strength.

Chapter Fourteen
Saturday Morning Strike

"Alex...Alex...Al-ex!"

Alex opened his eyes and realized he wasn't dreaming. His mom was calling him. "Yes, ma'am," he answered.

"Theodore is on the phone."

He yawned and looked at the clock and said, "6:00?" He went to the door and took the phone from his mom. He sat on his bed and said, "Hello?"

Theodore asked, "You're going to sleep all day?"

"Not with a friend like you," Alex joked back. "Why are you up so early?"

Theodore said, "I've been up for an hour. I've waited so long, and now, finally, I'm going bowling with you and the other guys, today!"

Alex asked, "Do you need us to pick you up?"

No," said Theodore, "My aunt and uncle are taking me. Our families are going to watch us bowl. Isn't that cool? If I knew the other guys numbers I'd call them, too."

"Get their numbers while we're bowling," suggested Alex.

"That's a good idea. Well, don't be late," said Theodore, and then added, "Hey, how are you going to bowl with a sore hand?"

Alex looked at his hand and said, "I've got an idea and if it doesn't work, I'll figure out something else."

Theodore said, "Don't forget to eat a good breakfast. You'll need the extra energy to beat me."

"Okay, I'll see you in a little while," said Alex.

Theodore said, "See, ya!"

Alex hung up the phone and got dressed. As he passed his parent's room his mom said, "It's a little early for your friends to be calling."

"Yes, ma'am," he answered then asked, "What's for breakfast?"

Mom said, "Breakfast! It's too early to be eating!"

Hearing Alex, Leora ran from her room and asked, "Mom, what's for breakfast?"

Mom covered her face and yawned.

Dad looked at his wife and asked, "Dear, what's for breakfast?"

Mom sat up and playfully swung a pillow at her husband. He dodged the pillow and suggested, "How about restaurant food?"

"Now, that's the best idea I've heard all day," Mom said.

Three hours later, Alex and his family were sitting in a restaurant, eating breakfast. He took the last bite of food and looked at his watch and said, "It's 9:15. We have to be at the bowling alley at 10:00."

"We're going to be there on time. Don't worry," Mom said.

"I can't wait," Alex said. He tried to sit still but kept finding himself tapping his feet on the floor or drumming out a rhythm with his fingers.

Mom ate her breakfast as she spoke to her husband. She kept being distracted by Alex's fingers drumming on the table. She grabbed his hands and said, "You're making me nervous."

Alex put his hands in his pockets but before long, his feet were dancing again.

"Alex! Please stop kicking the table," Mom said. "You're spilling everything."

Alex said, "Sorry." He used his napkin to clean up the spilled orange juice and milk. He looked at his watch again and announced, "It's 9:35."

"He sounds like a coo-coo clock," said Leora with a grin. Everyone laughed at Leora's joke, including Alex.

Dad said, "We are only five miles away from the bowling alley. We are going to get there with plenty of time to spare."

A few minutes later everyone was finished eating. The waitress stopped and left the ticket on the table and smiled as she continued stopping at other tables. Dad pulled money from his wallet and Alex sprang up from his chair. Mom and Dad chuckled as they stood up.

The Dog Was Adopted Too

Mom took Leora's hand and joined Dad in following Alex out of the restaurant door. Dad backed the van from the parking space. In a few minutes, they came to a stop at the bowling alley, and Alex was the first to hop out of the van and sprint toward the building.

He looked at his watch and said, "Fifteen minutes early. Thanks Dad."

Alex waited for his family, and together they entered the bowling alley. His excitement level piqued when he heard the sounds of bowling balls hitting pins. He looked around searching for his friends. Leora tapped his arm and pointed to Mr. Walker who was talking to Theodore, his aunt, and his uncle.

Alex said, "There they are," and hurriedly led his family to join their friends.

"I saw them first," complained Leora.

"I know dear," Mom said. "That's alright."

Mr. and Mrs. Bennett smiled and warmly greeted Alex's parents. Leora then invited them to sit at their table. Theodore jumped up and moved to an empty table, Alex sat across from him and they began talking excitedly.

Theodore said, "I've already given Mr. Walker the tickets. Come see the ball I've chosen and we'll find one for you." It took a few minutes but finally a "left-handed" ball was located for Alex. Theodore asked, "Have you bowled left-handed before?"

"No," answered Alex, "but I guess I'll learn."

Mr. Walker said, "Boys, go warm up at lanes five and six while you wait."

The boys hurried to the lanes. After throwing several gutter balls, Theodore made a point. He bowled again and knocked down two more pins.

Alex said, "Now, it's my turn." Carefully he lifted the ball with his left hand, and with both hands held it under his chin as he walked toward the lane. He swung the ball behind him and awkwardly hurled it forward. He watched as it flew two feet into the air, bounced loudly, and rolled straight for the pins. He shouted, "Yes!" The ball rolled a bit to the right, tapped a pin, wobbled down the gutter and disappeared. The pin rocked back and forth then straightened back up like a victorious soldier. Alex punched at the air.

From behind, he heard, "You're not throwing a baseball, you

know." He turned and saw all of the boys and their families standing and applauding for him. He laughed, bowing deeply and trotted back, giving each boy a high-five.

All of the boys began bowling. Their parents sat at nearby tables and chatted, occasionally cheering and applauding as they watched their children. All of the other siblings sat at tables and talked or played games that had been supplied by their parents. Some of the kids cheered for their bowling brothers as they made strikes.

Joshua, who hadn't hit a pin yet, had been watching a team who was bowling well. At his turn, he held the ball just under his chin and posed like the players he had been watching. When he had the pins "in his sights," he bent his knees slowly and stepped forward with ever increasing momentum. Concentrating on his form, he accidently crossed over the foul line into forbidden territory. As graceful as a ballet dancer, he lifted the ball behind him, swung his arm forward and gently released it. Unaware that oil had been applied to the lane, his feet slipped and flew up in the air before him. He and the ball hit the wooden floor at the same moment. He landed in a seated position and turned in slow circles following the ball down the lane. He finally stopped, but the ball continued rolling and made a beautiful strike.

The other bowlers jumped to their feet when Joshua fell and were nearly screaming with cheers and laughter when the ball made the strike. He tried to get up into a crawling position, but his hands and knees kept slipping. He looked like a newborn calf trying to stand for the first time. Finally, he scooted close to the gutter and grabbing the edge, rolled over into it. He managed to get his feet together, and by walking heel to toe like a tightrope walker, he made it back to the main floor. The room burst out in applause, cheers, and whistles. Joshua grinned broadly and raised his arms in victory and the cheers boomed louder.

Someone handed him a towel, and he wiped the oil from his hands and clothes. Michael laughed as he handed him the ball and said, "You'll do anything to knock those pins over, won't you?"

"You're just jealous," Joshua teased back.

The bowling continued for another hour. When the game was over, the boys gathered in a tight circle to compare scores. The printout revealed that Joshua was the winner with the highest score of 72 and Alex had the lowest score of 51.

The Dog Was Adopted Too

The group cheered as Mr. Walker gave Joshua a first place ribbon and then gave Alex a bottle of candy labeled "Bowl Better Pills." Everyone tried to see the ribbon and the pills until someone shouted, "Pizza is ready." The hungry bowlers raced to the dining area.

Theodore caught up with Alex, and pushing him with his shoulder, guided him down the hall to the right.

At first, Alex resisted, but then he allowed Theodore to lead him along a wall.

He asked, "Where are we going?"

"I'll show you," Theodore said as he led Alex down the hall.

Chapter Fifteen
Saturday Morning
The Short Hallway

Theodore led Alex past the restrooms and a door with a sign that read "Employees Only." The boys came to a short hallway on the left with a sign above it that read "Kitchen." Alex could see two beams of light shining from a door on the left wall at the end of the hall. Alex thought it looked like headlights from a car. The boys quietly trotted down to two shiny swinging-type metal doors. The beams of light came from two round viewing windows, one built into each door. Alex looked through one of the windows. Directly across the room from where he and Theodore were standing, Alex could see another set of doors that were identical to the ones that they were looking through.

They watched as a waitress removed a white box from the refrigerator and placed it on a counter. She opened the box and removed a white cake which was decorated with blue and green icing and had a figurine standing in the middle. She picked up the cake and a cake knife and put them in the center of a cart. She got ice cream from the freezer, several spoons, bowls and napkins, then put them on the cart next to the cake. Carefully she opened the ice cream and began spooning it into the bowls. When she was finished she put everything away. Gently she pushed the cart through the swinging doors. When the doors opened, Alex could see his friends and their families sitting in the dining area as they were being served their food.

Alex said, "Theodore, I'm hungry. That cake looked delicious. What are we waiting for?"

Theodore opened the right door and motioning to Alex, he said, "Well, come on in then."

Theodore stopped Alex in the middle of the room. "Are we eating here?" asked Alex.

"You'll see," said Theodore. Alex looked around the room, so he didn't see Mr. Walker when he waved at Theodore through one of the windows from the dining area side. Theodore tugged on Alex's arm and said, "Come on."

Alex jokingly scolded, "You sure are bossy all of a sudden! Stop! Go! Stop! Go!"

Theodore chuckled as he opened the door to the dining area and pushed Alex through. When Alex entered the room everyone stood up, and shouted, "Surprise!" and began applauding.

Alex abruptly stopped, which caused Theodore to run into his back. Alex was truly surprised as he looked at the smiling faces around him. He saw the cart with the decorated cake which now had glowing candles on top of it. When the applause stopped some of the boys followed Alex as he walked over to the cake. The cake's figurine was a boy in a bowling position getting ready to throw a bowling ball. Below the bowler was written, "Happy Birthday Alex."

His head snapped up and he looked at Theodore with a surprised expression and said, "My birthday isn't for two more weeks." All the boys and their families laughed.

Theodore said, "I know. I figured this would be a good time to surprise you."

Alex laughed and said, "It worked! How did you know when it would be my birthday?"

"It was a really hard thing to find out," Theodore said. "I asked your mom."

Alex smiled as he looked at his mom who winked at him. She was sitting at a booth between Alex's dad and Leora. All three were happily smiling and clapping their hands.

Michael said loudly, "Come on Foster. Blow out the candles and let's get this party going."

Theodore said, "Wait! We have to sing the birthday song."

Theodore pointed to Mr. Walker who stepped to the center of the room and with the strong voice of a choir member, began to lead the singing. The room was filled with, "Happy birthday to you; Happy birthday to you; Happy birthday dear Alex; Happy birthday to you."

Alex, wearing a wide grin, took a deep breath, puckered his lips, leaned over, and blew out all but one of the candles. Theodore quickly bent over and puffed the final flame out before Alex could get to it. Alex said, "Dude! You messed up my wish!" Everyone laughed while most of them sat down and returned to their eating.

A waitress wheeled in a cart beside Alex. Several gifts were piled on it. He smiled wider and said, "Thanks guys."

Alex's mom and Theodore's aunt walked over to the cart with the cake. Mrs. Foster said, "Go eat your lunch boys." The two ladies cut the cake and Leora walked from table to table serving the cake and ice cream to each guest. Alex joined his dad, and Theodore sat next to his uncle. Alex looked at Theodore and gave him two thumbs up. Theodore bit his pizza and lifted it toward Alex as a salute.

When Alex was finished eating, he rose and went to the gift cart. He began opening his gifts as if he were a paper shredder. All of the boys and some of the parents gathered around him. He opened each gift and thanked each giver. The gifts were passed around so everyone could see them. Often someone commented, "Cool," or "I'd like to have one of those."

Alex thanked everyone and the adults returned to their tables. Mrs. Foster and Mrs. Bennett gathered up the torn wrapping paper as the waitress began clearing the empty tables.

Alex asked his friends, "Did all of you know about this party?"

Derick said, "No, I always carry a gift in my back pocket, just in case I find a birthday party." Everyone laughed at Derick's humor.

Kevin said, "Let's play some of the games." The boys excitedly hurried to the game room.

Alex pulled Theodore aside and said, "I thought that I was supposed to be helping 'you' to be happy."

Theodore smiled and replied, "You 'have' helped me a lot. Two weeks ago, I couldn't have imagined feeling this happy or having a bunch of friends like this. I wanted to thank you, and this birthday party was my opportunity to pay you back."

Alex said, "Thanks," and gave Theodore a high-five. Then they joined the rest of the group.

After a while, the families began calling their children together. Everyone began saying their good-byes. Joshua was teased about his "rare" bowling form, and Alex was encouraged to get another bottle of "Bowl Better Pills." Soon Alex, Theodore, and their families were the only ones remaining. Mr. and Mrs. Bennett explained to Mr. Walker how much his Sunday school class meant to Theodore and thanked him for allowing the kids to bowl.

Patting Theodore on the shoulder, Mr. Walker said, "You're welcome, but it was Theodore's hard work that earned the passes."

Mr. Walker stood by the front exit door and watched the two families as they helped carry Alex's gifts to the van. As the two vehicles drove away, he breathed a prayer of praise to God for His loving care. Smiling with pleasure, he turned, letting the door close behind him. He returned to his other customers.

Alex sat in the back seat of the van, looking out the window. Mom asked, "Is this the same boy that couldn't sit still this morning?"

Alex smiled and said, "I can't believe how much fun I had today."

Leora said, "I did, too. I laughed when Joshua slipped."

They laughed and talked the entire drive home. When the van stopped in the driveway, Leora was the first to jump out. She jumped, twirled around, and pretended to throw bowling balls as Mom, Dad and Alex removed the gifts from the van. Leora followed Dad to the house. Dad turned the key in the door lock, and Leora squeezed passed him and raced through the half opened door. Dad allowed mom to go in before him. As Alex followed his parents inside, he heard the telephone ringing. Leora shouted, "I'll get it!" She picked up the phone and said, "Hello...Wait a minute...Alex, its Theodore."

Alex took the phone and said, "Hello?"

"Can you meet me at the park?" Theodore questioned.

"Let me find out." He turned and asked, "Dad, may I meet Theodore at the park?"

Dad looked at the clock and said, "Sure, but don't be gone all day."

"I can go," said Alex. "What time should I be there?"

"Can you leave right now?" asked Theodore.

"Sure, I'll see you at the gazebo in a few minutes," replied Alex.

Chapter Sixteen
Saturday Afternoon
The Mud Story

Theodore was in the gazebo, leaning on the railing with his back to Alex.

When Alex walked up the steps, he said, "Hi. What's up?"

Theodore turned around and sat on one of the seats that had been built into the structure. He said "Hey, Alex. I called you because I have some questions."

Alex sat on the other end of the bench from Theodore. He sat up straight and tall as he pretended to proudly polish his fingernails against his shirt and asked, "Okay, what do you need to know from the genius?"

Theodore said, "Well, that's why I wanted to talk to you. You seem to... I don't know... I guess you seem to be smart."

Alex blinked and stared at Theodore as he realized that the boy was not trying to be funny. "Smart! I'm smart about what?" Alex smirked.

"First, I need to tell you some things before I start asking questions." He looked away and continued, "I have a brother named Ronnie. Our parents were killed in a car accident, and we were sent to live with two different families that we didn't know."

Alex was surprised at the serious nature of Theodore's personal revelation. "I'm sorry," he said softly.

"For a long time, I was sad and lonely. I didn't go anywhere but to school. I didn't know anybody there. Then I started going to church, but I didn't know anyone there either. I just didn't know how to make

The Dog Was Adopted Too

friends."

Alex's guilt about the way he had felt about Theodore in the past hung over him like a dark rain cloud. He meekly said again, "Uh, I'm sorry."

Theodore said, "But then I got to know you. I'm glad that I did, because you helped me to see how wrong my thinking had been. That's one of the things that I want to talk to you about."

Some noisy younger kids ran up on the gazebo, then ran in circles chasing each other.

Theodore said, "Let's go to the pond." The two friends talked as they left the noise and strolled to the quiet shade, then sat on a bench near the water.

Theodore continued, "Frances had told me a story about a broken doll. Yesterday, we talked to her about Peter walking on the water. It made me do a lot of thinking." He hesitated, looked up at Alex, and with a slight smile said, "But the best thing was when you told me that my aunt and uncle had agreed to let me live with them before my parents died. You told me to ask them about it and I did."

Alex straightened up. His eyes widened as he asked, "You did! What'd they say?"

Smiling, Theodore said, "Well, It's more about what they gave me." He stood up and reached into the bulging back pocket of his jeans. He pulled, twisted, and finally with a big yank produced an over-stuffed man's wallet. Putting it on the bench between them, he opened it and several cards, papers, and pictures slid out. He picked up the top picture and gave it to Alex. The photo was of eight people: six adults, one baby, and a young boy.

With surprise, Alex said, "Hey! This must be the picture I heard your aunt talking about!" Touching it with his index finger, he said, "That's your uncle and aunt. Is that you?"

Theodore said, "Yeah, that's me standing between my mom, Christine, and my dad, Raymond. They're holding my baby brother, Ronnie. The two other people are Aunt Barbara and Uncle Ralph. Ronnie is living with them. Uncle Samuel said that he and Aunt Betty have been saving the wallet for me and waiting for the time that I asked questions." Pointing, he said, "Turn it over and read the back."

Alex flipped over the photo and read, "Theodore and Ronnie: This photo was made the day that your Aunt Betty, Uncle Samuel, Aunt

Barbara and Uncle Ralph agreed to raise you if something happens to both of us. They all love you very much. Love, Mom and Dad." Looking at the front of the photo again, Alex said, "That's cool!"

"Aunt Betty told me that our families used to live close to each other. She said that they saw me almost every day as I was growing up. Aunt Barbara, Uncle Ralph, and their son, Greg, lived near us, too. Greg took the picture. That's why he's not in it.

"Uncle Samuel said that we used to do all kinds of things together, and he and Aunt Betty spent the whole evening telling me stories. We used to have a lot of fun," Theodore said as he smiled. Theodore looked at the photo again and said, "My parents were great. It was nice talking about them with people who remember them, too."

Alex smiled and returned the photo. He wasn't sure if Theodore was going to laugh or cry. He asked, "Do you remember doing the things your aunt and uncle told you about?"

"I remember some things, but I didn't remember who the people were," Theodore said as he repacked the wallet and pushed it back into his pocket. "Uncle Ralph's and Uncle Samuel's jobs made them move away when I was little. That's why I don't remember much about them."

"Did your aunt and uncle ever call or visit?" Alex asked.

"Yeah," Theodore said, "They used to send cards." Excitedly, Theodore bounced in his seat and added, "I almost forgot to tell you! We're going to visit Ronnie in a few weeks."

"Wow! That's great," Alex said loudly as he patted Theodore on his shoulder.

"This morning, I felt almost as happy as I used to feel," said Theodore as the toe of his shoe dug into the ground. He continued, "But, I still need to ask you a question." Looking more serious, he said, "Last night, my aunt and uncle said something that made me start wondering."

Alex asked, "Wondering about what?"

"Well," Theodore began as he watched his shoe cover the hole it had dug, "when I talked about missing Mom and Dad, Aunt Betty said that I would see them again, someday. I asked her what she meant, and Uncle Samuel said that all Christians go to heaven and when I get there, I'll see them." Theodore looked up at Alex and said, "That's what my question is about. My dad and mom took Ronnie and me to church,

The Dog Was Adopted Too

but I don't remember what they told me about being a Christian. I don't know if I did what they told me or not. How do I know if I'm a Christian?"

Alex asked. "Well, do you know what a Christian is?"

Theodore said, "I guess a Christian is a person that acts really good. Last night, when I was wondering about it, I thought that maybe God gives something like grades on a report card so you can, sort of, graduate into heaven. I was hoping that I've been good more than I've been bad, so I would average a grade of 'C'. Then, I worried that maybe you have to make a 'B' or worse yet, everything has to be an 'A'. I don't know what to think."

Alex said, "You don't have to worry about that kind of stuff to get into heaven."

Theodore asked, "Well, what's it about, then? What do I have to do?"

Alex said, "When I asked about becoming a Christian, my parents told me that it's all about Jesus, not about me. My mom told a story to me that helped. You want to hear it?"

Theodore said, "Sure."

Alex said, "It's called 'The Mud Story*.'"

Theodore said, "Mud?"

"Yeah," Alex said. "Mom told me that the mud was the same thing as sin in the story."

"I was wondering what mud had to do with being a Christian," smiled Theodore.

"When I get through with the story, you'll see," Alex said.

"Okay," said Theodore, "Go on."

Alex began, "A little boy and his dad were happy in a beautiful, clean, dry house. One day it rained a lot, and the yard got very muddy. When the sun came out, the little kid went outside to play. After a while, he got hungry and went back inside. He didn't notice the big chunks of mud on his feet. He tracked mud everywhere that he went. His dad saw the muddy floor and told the boy to go outside.

"The boy asked, 'Why do I have to go out? I'm hungry.'

"His dad told him that if he let him bring mud in, soon no one would be able to tell the inside of the house from the outside. The boy said he understood and went back out while the dad cleaned up the mess.

"When the dad finished cleaning up the mud, he picked up a robe and went outside to check on his son. He saw the boy in the yard trying to clean the mud from his shoes. Each time he wiped the mud from one shoe it got muddy again while he tried to clean the other one. His hands got muddy. He brushed his hair from his face and smeared mud across his forehead. Before long, he was muddy from head to foot.

"He shouted, 'Dad, help me. I can't get clean by myself.'

"His dad walked down to the lowest step and said, 'Come here son.'

"Without getting muddy, the dad wrapped the robe around his son and carried him inside. He bathed him in clean water, dressed him in clean clothes and fed him a good warm meal. Soon the happy boy was sleeping safely in his dad's arms, inside his dad's house.

"Mom told me that we're like the boy in the muddy yard. He couldn't get clean because the mud was everywhere, and he wasn't able to get out of it. Mom said we can't get rid of our sins by ourselves either, because the temptation to sin is everywhere in the world. Like the little boy who couldn't get away from the mud, we can't get away from our sins."

"So, God cleans the sin off of us and we can go to heaven?" asked Theodore.

"Well," said Alex, "Do you remember what the boy told his daddy when he called for help?"

"You mean when he told his dad that he couldn't clean himself up?" Theodore asked.

"That's right. Well, we have to ask Jesus to clean us up. In real life, we have to ask Jesus to forgive us from our sins. And He will," Alex explained.

"How?" asked Theodore.

"Remember when the dad used clean water to get rid of the mud? Mom said that Jesus is the clean Living Water that takes away our sin. She said that He is the only one who can," commented Alex.

"Okay, so we have to ask Jesus to forgive us first?" questioned Theodore.

Alex pulled his wallet from his pocket and a little paper book fell out of it and slipped through one of the spaces in the park bench. Alex put his wallet back into his pocket and reached under the bench to pick up the little book.

The Dog Was Adopted Too

Theodore asked, "What is that?"

Alex said, "This is a tract. It teaches about the Bible. Have you ever read John 3:16?"

"I don't know," replied Theodore.

Alex opened the tract and read, "For God so loved the world that He gave His only begotten Son, that whosoever believes in Him should not perish but have everlasting life."

"I remember! That verse says that God loved us and sent Jesus, to die for us. All we have to do is believe in Him and we can go to heaven." said Theodore.

"Right," encouraged Alex.

Theodore said, "I remember Mama telling me that Jesus died on the cross and that when He was buried, He didn't stay dead."

Alex smiled and said, "That's right." He gave the tract to Theodore and pointed to I Corinthians 15: 3b-4.

"What does the 'B' mean?" asked Theodore.

"It tells you to start reading in the second part of the verse," explained Alex.

"Okay." Theodore began reading, "Christ died for our sins according to the scriptures, and that He was buried, and that He rose again the third day according to the scriptures."

"After the crucifixion, Jesus had been seen by lots of people before He went back to heaven," Alex said. "Now, if we believe that He lived, died for our sins, and rose from the grave, we can go to heaven to be with Him, forever."

Theodore asked, "How did Jesus get to heaven?"

"He floated up while a lot of people watched Him," Alex responded.

"Jesus floated up to heaven?" asked Theodore.

"Yes, He did, and one day He's coming back," answered Alex.

"Is that when I'm going to get to see my parents?" ask Theodore.

"That's what Mom told me. She said that seeing Jesus is more important than anything. That was why Jesus let Himself get crucified. He is the only way that we can get to heaven and see God," stated Alex.

"Did Jesus know that all those bad things were going to happen to Him? I can't see anybody getting crucified on purpose!"

"Well, He did do it on purpose," Alex answered. "Jesus died for our sins because we couldn't do it ourselves. He did it so we could believe in

Him, and what He did on the cross, so we could become Christians." Alex took the tract again and turned a page. He silently read down the page, then put his finger on a line of words. He turned it toward Theodore and said, "Mom told me that Jesus is like a door that leads us to God. Read this."

Theodore took the tract and read John 14:6, "Jesus saith unto him, 'I am the way, the truth, and the life: no man cometh unto the Father, but by me.'"

"See, Jesus is the only way to get to God," Alex said.

Theodore gave the tract back to Alex and asked seriously, "What if I can't remember everything that you've told me?"

"You don't have to know everything all at once," explained Alex.

Theodore asked, "Well, that's good. So, what's the first thing that I have to do?"

Alex returned the tract to Theodore and said, "Look what it says." Pointing to the back of the tract he read, "Say a prayer and tell God: 1) I am a sinner and am sorry for all my sins; 2) I believe God's Son, Jesus, died for my sins and rose from the grave; 3) I want to ask You Jesus to be my Savior; 4) I will tell others what Jesus did for me. When you pray this prayer, He will forgive you of all your past sins, and you will have a new home in heaven one day."

Theodore looked surprised and asked, "You mean that I have to tell people about this?"

"Sure. God wants everybody to know how to become a Christian," Alex answered. "Mom said that telling others about Jesus is a Christian's job. She told me that I should never be ashamed of Jesus." He stood up when he heard a buzzing sound and saw a streetlight blink on.

Theodore said. "Okay. Thanks. I guess I have more to think about." He handed the tract back to Alex.

"Keep it." Alex said, "Show it to your aunt and uncle. They'll be able to help you understand even more. Oh, and Mom told me something else. She said that if Jesus did miracles and walked on water, He could have just come off the nails and left the cross any time. She also said that if we could go to heaven by being good enough, then Jesus would have been pretty silly for dying on the cross for nothing."

Theodore looked at the tract and said, "Jesus must have loved us a lot to do that."

Alex said, "Yep."

The Dog Was Adopted Too

"That's awesome!" Theodore said as he put the tract in the pocket of his pants. "See, I told you that you were smart."

Alex looked up as another street light flickered on and said, "Well, thanks. Do you want to walk back with me? It's getting dark."

"No, thanks," Theodore responded then asked, "How did you learn all of this about God?"

"My parents tell me stuff," said Alex, "and I learn more about the Bible at church."

"So I can learn all the things that you know?" asked Theodore hopefully.

"Sure. I'm still learning and so can you." Another light buzzed on and Alex said, "I have to go. See you in the morning." He turned and trotted up the path toward home.

"See ya." Theodore watched as Alex hurried away. He went to the edge of the pond and touched the water with his shoe. Ripples spread out in even circles, distorting the reflections. He thought about what Alex had told him. When he turned to go, his foot slipped and he fell in the moist soil. He got up, looked at the mud on his hands, pants, and shoes then brushed away as much as he could. He sat on the bench, and using a stick, scrubbed most of the mud from his shoes. As he scrapped at the mud, he noticed that the stick was almost "T" shaped, like a cross.

He wiped the mud from the stick and thought, "If I could get rid of my sins by myself, dying on the cross would have been a silly thing for Jesus to do."

He glanced up as another street light flashed on and placed the stick on the bench. He noticed the shadows from the tree branches as they moved in the breeze. His imagination made him see shapes moving among the tree trunks. He looked around and wished he had left for home sooner. He trotted down the path toward the next street light.

Chapter Seventeen
Saturday Evening
A Looming Figure

The time was later than Alex had realized, and he knew his parents were going to be upset with him. He walked briskly between the trees that lined the park trail toward his home. He looked around at the leaves blowing in the darkness. The street lights seemed to be farther apart and it was getting harder to see. He picked up his speed and wondered if it was as dark where Theodore was walking.

He thought about how much Theodore had changed in the last few days. A few months ago he showed up at school and then later, he had joined the Sunday school class. He had never talked to Alex or any of the boys, so no one had talked to him. Everything had been fine until he butted in and started winning the Sunday school contests. Alex and his friends had paid him back by really being rude and ignoring him. Alex remembered when Theodore had moved to the back of the class and had become even quieter. At the time, most of the class was glad of it. Now, the boys all regretted it.

Alex walked quickly while not paying much attention to the trail. As he refocused on the path, a movement in the bushes to his left distracted him. He glanced over and saw a bird flutter from a bush. He jerked his head back around just in time to see a low tree branch. He tried to duck, but it was too late. He felt a heavy thud to his forehead. He blinked, fell back and landed heavily on his backside. He started to get up, but heard something skid to a stop behind him. He jerked his throbbing head back making everything look upside down. He gasped in shock as he saw an inverted figure looming over him! He panicked and quickly crab-walked away from the shadowy figure!

"Are you alright?" Theodore asked while breathing heavily.

Alex let out a loud sigh of relief and whispered hoarsely, "Man, you almost scared me to death!"

Theodore trotted around to Alex's feet and reached down to help the dizzy boy up from the ground.

Theodore, almost panting said, "I saw you fall and was worried that you were hurt."

Alex took his concerned friend's hand and pulled himself upright. He rubbed his battered head and bent his arm to see what was stinging him. Through a ragged hole in his sleeve he could see his scraped but non-bleeding elbow.

He tried to close the hole in the ragged fabric over his elbow as he said, "A streetlight was behind you, and all I could see was a big shadow standing over me. I couldn't tell that it was you. At first you sort of looked like Big Foot."

"Me? I looked like Big Foot? You're the one who stumbled over his big clumsy feet!" stated Theodore with a teasing laugh.

"Hey," muttered Alex, "I didn't stumble. A tree branch hit my head and knocked me down."

Theodore asked with a laugh, "Is the tree okay? Getting hit by something as hard as your head could have hurt it."

"Oh, you're so funny!" said Alex with a smirk as he chuckled.

"Sorry," said Theodore, "I just couldn't resist poking fun at you."

"Go on funny boy," said Alex while rubbing his head again. He asked, "Why were you following me? I thought you were going home."

"I was," replied Theodore, "but I couldn't remember if I thanked you. Do you know how fast you walk? You should go out for track. I couldn't catch up with you!" Theodore pushed his hair back from his sweating forehead.

Alex laughed loudly and said, "You just smeared mud on your face."

Theodore looked at his muddy hands and laughed as he wiped the mud away with the back of his hand. "I slipped in the mud by the pond," admitted Theodore.

"So who's clumsy, now?" asked Alex.

"Let's just call it a tie," chuckled Theodore as he rubbed his hands together to remove as much mud as he could.

"Okay," replied Alex. "By-the-way, what were you wanting to thank me for?"

Theodore smeared the rest of the mud onto his pants leg, then looked up at Alex and said, "I need to thank you for coming to the park to talk to me. You were the first person in school or church to talk to me. Well, the first person our age anyway. You included me with the other guys at church on Wednesday night and then, at your house, you helped me to set up the bowling game. This morning, at the bowling alley, I had no clue about what I was doing, but I still had a lot of fun."

Both boys chuckled. Alex grew quiet and felt a twinge of guilt again, because he had been asked by Mr. Walker to help Theodore.

He looked away and said, "Don't worry about it. I had fun too."

Theodore said, "The day that I was at your house when we sat by the fireplace was the first time that I've had fun in a long while. It made me think of the times that my mom, dad, Ronnie and I used to do family things together. I just wanted to thank you for being my friend and for helping me to feel better."

Alex replied, "You gave me a birthday party today. I think you are caught up with saying thank you.

Alex stuck his hands in his pockets, looked down and kicked at a root that stood out of the ground. He said, "Theodore, I'm glad that we are friends. I really am, but I have to tell you something that's been bothering me."

Theodore, with a worried look on his face, asked, "What did I do?"

Alex looked up at Theodore, then back down at the ground, and slowly shook his head. He had seen Theodore's worried expression and wished he had stayed quiet. He said, "No, it's nothing."

Theodore said, "Look, you're my new best friend. If I've said or done something wrong, I want to fix it."

Alex pulled his hands from his pockets. He rubbed his index finger on the sore dog bite in the palm of his hand.

"New best friend!" he said to himself as his heart sank deeper. "No. It's me. I'm glad that we're friends, but I feel bad about something."

"What?" Theodore asked.

"It wasn't me. It was Mr. Walker that helped you." Alex stepped over to a tree and leaned his shoulder against it. He looked up at Theodore and began again. "Last Sunday morning, Mr. Walker asked me to help you to make new friends." Alex looked away and shrugged his shoulders. "I'm glad that he did, but I feel bad that you think that it was my idea."

"Oh, I know about that."

"You do? How?" Alex asked.

"I'd asked Mr. Walker to help me because I didn't have any friends, and I was lonely. I didn't know what he'd do but when you started talking to me and being friendly, I figured that he had asked you to be my friend. Later, when I asked him about it, he said that you had agreed to help me and I thanked him. Then, when you left me a few minutes ago, I remembered that I needed to thank you too. I really am glad that you helped me."

"Good." Alex straightened up and walked back onto the path. His heart began to feel lighter. "You don't know what a relief that is to me," he admitted. "I was afraid that someday you'd find out that it hadn't been my idea and be mad at me."

"It doesn't matter whose idea it was. I'm just glad that it all worked out the way that it did. Uncle Samuel said that he thought that God had a lot to do with it too."

"I do too," agreed Alex. He looked around and said, "Look how dark it has gotten. My house isn't too much further. Come with me and we'll take you home."

"Naw, that's alright. I can get home by myself," replied Theodore.

"No, come on. The way that you scared me has given me the creeps. You don't need to be roaming around by yourself in the dark. Someone or something might get after you."

Theodore looked around and said, "Yes, it is pretty dark. By the time I walk back home, my folks will probably be worried and have the police after me."

"We'll both be in trouble if we don't hurry." The two friends trotted together and soon were walking up the steps of Alex's house. The boys crossed the porch and walked through the living room to the kitchen. The house was empty.

Puzzled, Alex said, "I wonder where everybody is." He looked at the refrigerator and searched for a sticky note.

He said, "Mom and Dad usually leave a note for me if they think they won't be back before I get home. Hey, I saw the car in the garage. I hope they're alright."

Suddenly, the sound of Leora's laughter pierced the air and made both boys spin around. Alex and Theodore shouted in unison, "They're in the back yard!" and they ran to the patio door.

Alex slid the door open, and he and Theodore stepped outside. Alex's parents were sitting at the picnic table and were watching Leora and two of her friends. Alex noticed bugs buzzing around the two lights that lit up the yard. One girl was riding Leora's bike as Leora and the other girl were running on either side of it. The bike began to wobble. Leora and the other girl both slowed down to avoid getting run over. The bike steered toward the fence and crashed into a flower bush.

Mom groaned loudly. She and Dad jumped up and ran to the violently shaking bush. She reached in and pulled the girl free. Finding no serious scrapes, she hugged the whimpering girl as Leora and her other friend tried to comfort her, too.

Alex and Theodore ran to the bush and began pulling on the bike, but it wouldn't come loose. Dad reached over the bush, lifted the bike straight up, and put it on the ground in front of Leora.

"It looks alright. Thanks Dad," said Leora.

Mom said, "Okay girls. It's getting too dark and one of you may really get hurt. Put the bike in the garage then get cleaned up for bed."

Leora hopped onto the bike and rode toward the garage with the two girls running behind.

Alex saw the food on the table and told Theodore, "Let's eat." They hurried to the table and fixed two hamburgers. Alex picked up a chip and hungrily popped it in his mouth. Theodore sat down and scooped some chips into his plate. Alex poured two glasses of tea, sat down, and he and Theodore began to eat their burgers.

Dad chuckled as he and Mom joined the boys at the table. He asked his wife, "Do you think we will survive this night?"

Alex chuckled as he ate another potato chip, then washed it down with some tea. He said, "That girl would make a terrible medieval jouster."

"No kidding! She'd run out of horses really fast," laughed Theodore.

"She'd keep the medic's hopping, too!" Alex added as he ate more chips.

The Dog Was Adopted Too

Dad laughed, shook his head and said, "Boys, it's not nice to laugh at others people's misfortune."

"Alex wiped his mouth and said, "I know, but she drove into that bush just like she had aimed at it."

Mom chuckled and said to her husband, "You know dear, parents aren't supposed to laugh at the misfortune of others, either."

Dad smiled and said, "I know, but it did look funny."

Alex asked, "Why are those girls here?"

Mom said, "Leora just wanted some company so we let her invite Beth and Ginger to spend the night."

Dad asked, "What were you boys up to that made you so late?"

Alex said, "We talked until it was almost dark, so I asked Theodore to come here to see if you could take him home."

Mom said, "That's a good idea." Then looking at Theodore she asked, "You don't want to meet some bad guy in the dark, do you?"

Both boys laughed and Alex told about Theodore scaring him.

Dad looked at Alex and said, "Well, I'm glad that it turned out alright. Bad things can happen in the dark. That's why we expect Alex to be home early." He looked at Theodore and said, "Yes, we'll be glad to take you home. Go call your family and when you're finished eating we'll go."

Alex and Theodore went to the phone and Theodore called his family. When they came back, Alex's parents were clearing the table and were carrying the dishes back inside the house.

The boys sat down by their plates to finish eating. Theodore said, "Uncle Samuel sure was mad at me."

Dad walked back to the table and asked, "Who was mad at you?"

Theodore answered, "My folks. I called them like you told me too and got fussed at!"

Mom joined the group and asked, "Did Betty and Samuel know where you were?"

"Sure," said Theodore, then he added, "I ... actually all I told them was that I'd be back." He looked at Alex and said, "I was right. Aunt Betty said that she was about to call the police."

Mom asked Theodore, "Have you ever worried about someone?"

Theodore became defensive and, answering a little too sternly, said, "Well, sure. I worry about Ronnie and my parents all the time."

"I'm sorry. That's not what I meant," Mom apologized. "I was just trying to get you to understand Samuel and Betty's view point."

Theodore ate another chip and said, "Yes, Alex told me the other day, at the gazebo that it wasn't good for me to be off somewhere when no one knows where I'm going." He looked at Alex and said, "You looked like you were getting pretty worried when we got here and you couldn't find your folks."

Dad patted Alex on the shoulder and said, "Yes, we've had a lot of discussions about being late, haven't we son."

Yes," Alex laughed, "I guess your lectures could be called discussions."

"I guess I owe them an apology," admitted Theodore. "I wasn't very nice on the phone."

The boys finished eating and followed Dad to the truck. Mr. Foster put the truck in reverse and started to back out of the drive way. Mom and the three pajama-clad girls waved bye to them.

As they drove away, Theodore waved back at Alex's mom and the three girls. He said, "It sure must be nice to have a family."

Dad said, "You do have a family."

Theodore looked at Mr. Foster and said, "You're right. I guess I do."

Alex smirked and asked, "Did you forget?"

Theodore said, "No, but it's a new idea for me. Until the last couple of days I've always thought that I was a bother. I've never considered my aunt and uncle as a 'real' family."

"When we were all at the bowling alley your aunt and uncle looked like a real family. They acted just like all the other parents did," said Alex.

"They sure did," Theodore said thoughtfully. He smiled and then almost to himself he whispered, "Wow."

Alex asked Theodore, "Have you decided what to say at the 'Praise in the Park?'"

"No," said Theodore, "Have you?"

"I think I'll brag about our bowling day and the birthday party," Alex said as he proudly sat straight and tall.

"I know you won't be bragging about your bowling score," replied Theodore as he pushed his shoulder into Alex's arm.

Alex pushed back and said, "Well, at least I got a prize."

Theodore laughed loudly and said, "You sure did! Bowl Better

The Dog Was Adopted Too

Pills!" This made Alex laugh out loud.

Dad joined in on the laughter just as he pulled the truck into the Bennett's driveway. He chuckled and said, "We're here."

Mr. and Mrs. Bennett opened the screen door and walked onto the porch.

The two boys got out of the truck and chatted as they approached Theodore's house.

Theodore stopped before going up the steps. He looked at his aunt and uncle who were waving to Alex's dad. He thought about watching Alex's mom and the girls waving bye just a few minutes ago. He wondered, "What have I been thinking? They do love me." He turned toward Mr. Foster's truck and shouted, "Thank you for the ride home." Then to Alex he said, "See you tomorrow at church."

Alex said, "You'd better study for that contest. I'm ready this week."

Theodore chuckled and replied "We'll see how ready you are."

Alex trotted back to the truck and got in.

As his dad backed the truck out of the drive way, Alex rolled his window down and waved. He rolled the window back up and watched as Theodore trotted up the steps and stood next to his aunt and uncle. Alex said, "Dad, Theodore sure has changed this past week."

Dad glanced at Alex and replied, "A lot of changes have taken place with both of you boys this week."

"You're right. When we get home I want to talk to you and Mom about something that Theodore said today."

Chapter Eighteen
Saturday Night
This Is Really Great!

Alex jumped out of the truck and followed his dad inside the house. Mom had sent Leora and her friends to bed and she was sitting alone in the living room looking at a magazine. She stretched and yawned when her husband and her son entered the room. She put the magazine down and asked, "Well, what are my two men up to?"

Dad said, "Alex wants to talk to us."

Mom said, "Well, I'm all ears." She smiled at Alex and patted the couch cushion.

Alex sat down next to her and was quiet as he decided where to begin.

Dad sat in a chair across from his wife and his son. He asked, "What do you want to tell us?"

Alex looked from his mom to his dad and asked, "Do you remember how upset I was when Mr. Walker asked me to be Theodore's friend?"

Both parents nodded in response. Dad agreed, "Yes, you didn't seem to be very pleased."

"I wasn't. Everything is so different, now. I feel like Theodore has become one of my best friends and, just last week, I could hardly stand being in the same room with him."

"That's a good thing. God works that way," Mom said.

"I know," replied Alex, then he added, "but I feel so guilty because he is being so nice to me. When he met me at the park, the first thing

The Dog Was Adopted Too

he told me was that he wanted to ask me a question because he thinks that I'm so smart."

"He thinks you're smart about what?" Dad asked.

"He seems to think that I know a lot about the Bible. He started asking me about being saved. He said that his parents had taken him to church a lot, but he didn't know if he'd become a Christian."

"That's really an honor when your friends respect you that much," Mom stated, then asked, "What did you tell him?"

"I told him the 'Mud Story' that you had told me, and then I gave him a tract that I'd been given at church. He seemed to understand some of it, so I told him to go home and talk to his aunt and uncle. I've never done anything like that before. I sure was scared."

"I'm sure you did fine, son," said Dad.

"I hope so," Alex said. "But that isn't what's making me feel bad. You see, the night that Theodore and his folks came here for dinner, I heard Mrs. Bennett tell you about how hard they had tried to make Theodore happy after his parents died and he moved in with them. When I told Theodore about what I heard, he was surprised because he didn't think that they loved him at all. I told him to talk to his aunt and uncle about it when they went home."

"Did he ask Betty and Samuel about how they felt about him?" asked Dad.

"Yes, and they even gave him the wallet that had belonged to his dad. There was a picture in it that showed his parents, Ronnie and both sets of aunts and uncles. He even found out that he has a cousin named Greg."

"That must be the picture that Betty spoke about," said Mom.

"It is," said Alex.

He looked at his mom and dad and started to speak, but a lump in his throat kept him silent. He swallowed and rubbed his eyes with both open hands so his parents wouldn't see the tears that were trying to give away his emotions. He put his hands down and wiped them on his pant legs.

He said, "All that time I was mad because Theodore was winning the Sunday school contests, and he was living in a house with people that he believed didn't care for him." Alex swallowed again and continued, "He had no friends at all, and I couldn't see that he was sad. All I cared about was myself and what I wanted." Alex felt the lump return and he cleared his throat to chase it away. He continued, "I feel so ashamed that I had everything, and he felt like he had nothing." A tear escaped, hung on an eye lash then dropped to his cheek. He got up, crossed the room and looked out of a window.

"Alex," Dad said. "When we were coming home you commented about how much Theodore had changed. Do you remember that?"

Alex said, "Yes sir."

"Son, you have been doing a lot of changing too. You went from disliking Theodore to caring about his salvation and his family life. You were, I'm sorry to say, self-centered and now you have compassion for your new friend."

Mom added, "You've obeyed the great commission, and have shared Jesus."

Alex walked to the patio door and slid it open. He stepped outside and took a deep breath of fresh evening air. Mom and Dad joined him and sat in the chairs on the patio. Alex sat in a chair and watched the bugs that were swarming around the yard lights. He turned to his parents and asked, "What do I do now?"

Dad said, "God is at work in Theodore's heart. Salvation is God's job. He only expects us to help people to come to Jesus and you've done that. God will let you know what to do next."

Alex asked, "Should I mention it to him again?"

Mom said, "Sure you can talk to him about it. Ask God what to do. Since you told him to talk to his aunt and uncle, you can ask him if he did. Just don't be pushy. He respected you enough to talk to you about his salvation in the first place. Theodore will probably talk to you about it again."

Alex thanked his parents, then looked up at the moon and the stars and silently prayed for Theodore and his family.

At his home, Theodore looked at the moon and the stars through his bedroom window as he dried his freshly washed hair with a towel. He was glad that his aunt and uncle had accepted his apology for the way that he had spoken to them. He could hear them talking in the living room. He decided that this was the time to talk to them about his salvation. He said a silent prayer that God would help him know what to say. He turned away from the window and put his robe on over his pajamas. He saw the tract that Alex had given to him and put it in his robe pocket. He left his room and stopped in the kitchen to pour a glass of tea. His aunt and uncle were each sitting in their recliners and smiled as Theodore entered the room. He sat on the couch and put his glass on the coffee table. He sat quietly, trying to think of a way to ask them the questions that he felt were so hard.

Uncle Samuel noticed how still Theodore was. He asked, "Is everything alright, son?"

Theodore almost jumped when he heard the word son.

Aunt Betty asked, "Is anything wrong?"

Theodore said, "No, ma'am. I just need to talk to you and Uncle Samuel."

Aunt Betty made her recliner sit up straight and gave her full attention to Theodore. "Go ahead," she said, "you can talk to us about anything."

Theodore smiled at his aunt and said, "I don't know where to start." He looked down at his hands and twiddled his thumbs. Looking beyond his hands, he reached down and wiped away speckles of shower water from both of his bare feet. When he looked back up he saw that his aunt and uncle were still patiently waiting.

Uncle Samuel straightened his recliner and asked, "Does this have anything to do with the wallet that we gave you?"

"Well, a little bit," Theodore said quietly. "The note on the back of the picture helped me a lot."

He reached into his robe pocket and pulled out the tract that Alex had given him. It was wrinkled from being in his pants pocket. He laid the tract on his knee and tried to smooth it with his fingers.

"Was that in your dad's wallet?" asked Uncle Samuel.

"No," replied Theodore. "Alex gave this to me." He got up and gave the tract to his uncle then returned to the couch and sat down.

"Look Betty, it's a tract," Uncle Samuel said with pleasure.

"How nice," Aunt Betty said with a smile. "Did you read it?"

"Yes Ma'am. I asked Alex how I was supposed to know if I'm a Christian. He read that tract with me. He told me some things that his mom had told him. It all sounded good. Then he told me to talk to you about my salvation."

Uncle Samuel said, "I'm glad that he did. I've wanted to talk to you about salvation, but it just never seemed like the right time for it." He thumbed through the tract and read the "Sinner's Prayer" that was on the last page. He looked up at Theodore and asked, "Did you say this prayer and ask Jesus to be your Savior?"

"No sir. Alex read it to me, but he saw that it was getting late. That's when he told me to talk to you about it."

"Tell us what he said, and let's see if we need to add anything from that point," Aunt Betty suggested. Samuel handed her the tract. She looked through it as she listened to Theodore.

"Alex said that I didn't need to know everything all at once," Theodore stated.

"That's fine," Uncle Samuel said. "Read the Bible, go to church, and you will learn more as you get older."

"He told me a story about a little boy who got muddy. His dad had to clean him up before he could go inside the house. Alex said that the story means that we can't go into heaven with our sins. He said that if we did, soon heaven would be just like the sinful world. According to what he said, all I have to do is to tell God I'm sorry for my sins and ask Jesus to be my Savior. I'm not sure how to do that or just what it means."

Theodore put his feet on the coffee table and accidently knocked his glass of tea over. It rolled off the edge of the table and shattered on the tile floor. The tea followed the pattern created by the tile and raced in every direction. He lifted his feet from the table and folded his knees up against his chest. He wrapped his arms around his legs and watched as a stream of tea flowed under the couch. The pieces of glass glistened like diamonds everywhere on the floor.

Uncle Samuel threw a napkin over the main part of the broken glass. He reached for his slippers, put them on and hurried to the kitchen to get more napkins. Aunt Betty slid her slippers on and as she quickly left the room, she said. "You stay right there until we get this mess cleaned up. I don't want you to cut your feet."

Theodore closed his eyes and slowly lowered his head. Sarcastically he told himself, "This is really great." He lifted his head and with his eyes still closed, he said loudly, "I'm sorry."

CHAPTER NINETEEN
SATURDAY NIGHT
NEW BEGINNINGS

Uncle Samuel returned to the room carrying a roll of paper towels.

Aunt Betty carried a broom and dust pan as she returned to the room. "That's alright. We'll clean it up." She pulled Theodore's slippers from under her arm and tossed them to him.

Theodore said, "Give me some of the towels and I can clean up under the couch."

"No, no, no. We'll get it. I don't want you to get cut," said Uncle Samuel as he threw paper towels here and there over the tea and the glass.

Still holding his slippers in his hands, Theodore watched as the white paper soaked up the tea until each sheet was completely brown. Aunt Betty swept the wet towels and glass into a pile in the center of the sticky floor.

Some of the tea flowed from the pile of wet paper and had run back under the couch. He pointed to the floor and said, "The tea ran back under here."

Uncle Samuel held the dust pan as Aunt Betty swept the pile of soaked paper and broken glass onto the tray. He noticed the slippers in Theodore's hands and said, "Put on your slippers, climb over the back of the couch, and get a bucket of water, a mop, and a bottle of floor cleaner."

Theodore did as he was told and hurried to the laundry room. He easily found the mop and the bucket but not the cleaner. He turned to leave and saw several shelves that had been built onto the back of the door. He turned the light on and read the labels on the bottles and the cans. One of the bottles showed a picture of a mop on the label. He reached up for the bottle and his elbow knocked a small box to the floor. Some of the papers and envelopes dropped straight down and other papers glided farther away before landing on the floor. He gathered the items and as he put them back into the box he recognized the return address on one of the envelopes. He turned it to the light and recognized his mom's handwriting. He put the treasure in his pocket so he could ask what it was about.

Uncle Samuel went to the kitchen and poured three fresh glasses of tea. As he put Theodore's glass on the coffee table, he saw a speck of light next to Aunt Betty's chair. He went to investigate and found a piece of broken glass. He threw it in the trash and searched for others.

Theodore returned carrying the bucket, a mop, and a bottle. He saw that the couch had been pushed back and the tea had been dried up from the floor. Aunt Betty took the mop, the bottle, and the bucket from Theodore. She mopped and dried the floor, then swept it once more. No glass or stickiness was found, so she went to empty the mop bucket and put everything away.

The whole process had taken almost 20 minutes. Aunt Betty returned to the room and was drying her hands on a towel. Uncle Samuel was already seated in his chair and Theodore was once again sitting back on the couch. Aunt Betty sat down in her recliner, folded the towel, and let out a loud, long "Whew!"

"Now, back to what we were talking about," said Uncle Samuel. "You were telling us that you wanted to know what it means to accept Jesus as your Savior."

"Yes, I'm worried about the sinning part. I told Alex that I thought that sins were graded by how many good things and bad things that you've done. Alex said that I don't need to worry about that kind of thing. That's when he told me the story about the boy who got muddy and his dad wouldn't let him come into the house. He said that the dad cleaned the mud off because the boy couldn't do it himself. He said the dad was like God and the mud was like sin."

The Dog Was Adopted Too

"That sounds sort of like the parable of the prodigal son," said Uncle Samuel. "It shows the relationship between God the Father and the rebellious son. Just like the dad took care of the boy's mud problem, God is always waiting for us to ask for forgiveness so He can take care of our sin problem. That makes us all like the prodigal son."

"How long do sins last? I mean, when do they not count against you anymore?" Theodore asked softly.

"Both questions have the same answer," replied Aunt Betty. "Sins last until you ask God to forgive you for them. Once you have God's forgiveness, then they don't count against you anymore."

Theodore was obviously worried as he looked from his aunt to his uncle and asked, "How bad does a sin have to be to keep me from going to heaven?"

"Sinning is doing the opposite of God's will," answered Uncle Samuel. "God is so serious about sin that He sent His Son, Jesus, to pay the punishment for your sins. If you never accept Jesus as your Savior and you have only one sin, that one sin would keep you out of heaven."

"Oh," replied Theodore.

Uncle Samuel asked, "Have you been asking God to forgive your sins?"

"I don't remember," replied Theodore. Then scratching an imaginary itch by his ear, he looked up and said, "Well, actually that's not true. I do remember some things that I did, but back then I didn't know that I needed forgiveness. I guess that's why I'm so worried about it now."

Theodore sat up straight and hurriedly said, "I mean these things were a while ago. I've learned my lesson. I've been pretty good since I've been living with you. Well, I guess that isn't true either. I have been disobeying you and telling you stories to keep myself out of trouble." He shrugged his shoulders and sighed. He looked down at the floor and added, "I don't know what to do."

"You said that you learned your lesson. What do you mean?" asked Aunt Betty.

Theodore looked up and said, "When Ronnie and I were living at our foster home, we were put in a new school. It seemed everyone was talking about the great things that they did every weekend. You know what I mean? Everyone had parents and was always riding bikes, traveling, going to parties, bowling, fishing, skiing, and other fun stuff like that. They always laughed and teased each other, but no one ever talked to me. I didn't fit in because I never talked about my family. I mean, how could I talk about something that I didn't have anymore?"

Theodore noticed a new glass of tea on the coffee table. He picked it up, took a sip and watched the ice cubes as they floated in a circle. He put the glass down, cleared his throat and continued. "I started telling stories about the great things that I used to do with my family. Of course, I made it sound like it was happening right then. It worked, and soon I had a few friends. I told them everything that I could remember but, after a while, I had to start making up stories. I told them that I had trophies."

He looked from his aunt to his uncle and confessed, "I even said that I had blue ribbons from all the fishing rodeos that my dad and I had won. The kids wanted to see one of them, so I asked my foster mom to drop me off at the mall. I went to the trophy shop and chose a small one that had a shiny fish on it. I walked around for a few minutes before putting it in my pocket. When I left the store I set off the alarm. I would have gotten caught, but the sales clerk stopped another boy instead of me. I stepped around the corner and went to a restaurant. I was so scared.

Uncle Samuel had a concerned look on his face. He said, "You could have gotten in a lot of trouble if you had gotten caught."

"I know," said Theodore. "I had never been a thief before. It bothered me so bad that I had trouble sleeping that night. The trophy had made some of the boys jealous of me. I was so pleased with myself. It was great having friends again! I told about our big fancy house, our expensive cars, our boats, our rod-n-reels. Eventually, the stories got so big that the guys started doubting me. I had to do something. I stole a really cool fishing lure from my foster dad and told the guys how my dad and I had bought it on one of our trips. That did the trick! I felt bad about stealing and lying, but I couldn't stop myself. I wish I had stopped because soon they all wanted to come over and see everything that I had. That was a big problem, of course, because I didn't have any of those things."

Uncle Samuel interrupted and said, "My mom used to say, 'What a tangled web we weave, once we practice to deceive.'"

"You're right about that. I felt like I was caught in a web and couldn't get loose. I had to start making up more lies about why the boys couldn't come over to my house. You know things like, my dad's boss was coming over; my mom didn't like company; we had another trip coming up; or I had to take my horse to another competition and wouldn't be home." Theodore moved his hands as if something exploded. "Then one day everything blew up. My lies caught up with me when somebody saw me get off the bus and go into a regular house."

"I can imagine that didn't go over very well," added Uncle Samuel.

"No it didn't. The story spread like a wild fire. Soon it seemed that everybody knew that I was just a regular guy living in a regular house with a regular car. Everyone looked at me really mean so I guess they knew that I had no boats or any of the other things that I had bragged about."

Theodore drank more tea and stirred the ice cubes with his finger as he continued. "Well, I knew I was in real trouble when the guys came to my house one day and asked if I could go play ball with them. I told them that I couldn't go. Things got worse when my foster mom made me go. She thought it was good that I was finally getting out with friends." Theodore took another sip and put the glass down again. He saw the concerned expressions on the faces of his aunt and uncle and reluctantly continued.

"The guys walked with me down the street. When we got to a wooded area one of the boys pushed me through some bushes that grew behind a shed. The guys were really mad and ganged up on me. They pushed me around and asked why I had lied. I tried to explain to them, but they didn't want to listen. They shoved me down and told me not to bother them anymore. They disappeared through the bushes and never spoke to me again. I never had another friend after that."

Aunt Betty looked sad and said, "I'm sorry that happened."

Theodore sighed and shrugged his shoulders. "That's why, when I moved here, I didn't want to have any friends at this school because I didn't want to make the same mistake again. Theodore looked up and said, "Now, after all this time, I've got friends again and I thought everything was fine. Now I think I'm in a worse fix than I ever knew I could be."

"Why do you say that?" asked Aunt Betty.

"When I was a kid, I knew that lying and stealing were wrong," confessed Theodore, "but I didn't know that it was something that would stick with me forever. I sure didn't know it had anything to do with heaven. I mean, I knew that God didn't like it, but I didn't know how much He didn't like it."

"What did you think about God and heaven?" asked Aunt Betty.

"When I was little I thought heaven was a place where angels played harps while sitting on clouds. You know, like they show in cartoons." Theodore chuckled as he shook his head. "When I saw big ragged looking clouds, I used to think that my parents and the angels were hanging over the edge watching what I was doing."

Theodore looked seriously at his aunt and uncle and said, "Now I'm finding out that all the bad things that I had done back then are still with me. I can't change my past! I can't go back and find all of those guys that I lied to. If I did apologize to them they probably wouldn't forgive me anyway." Theodore leaned over, putting his elbows on his knees and hiding his face in his hands.

"I doubt that God would forgive me either." Without looking up, he shook his head as if to say no and asked, "So, what am I supposed to do?"

Uncle Samuel said, "Let me ask you a question. Why did you say you were sorry for breaking the glass? Was it because you didn't want to face punishment?"

Speaking through his hands he replied, "No. I really am sorry. I didn't mean to break it."

"Yes, I know you didn't," said Uncle Samuel. "I didn't sense anger or rebellion from you. God knows your heart better than anyone does, Theodore. He knows when you are naughty or nice, as they say about Santa Clause."

Theodore chuckled and sat up. He wiped at his wet eyes and looked at his uncle and waited for him to continue.

"Now, if God knows that you plan to break another glass, then He also knows that you are not really sorry. The same is true about your sins of lying and stealing. If you are really sorry and don't ever want to do any of that again, He knows that your heart has changed. And if you ask Him to forgive you and you really mean it, then He will forgive you. He erases your sin."

Theodore gave a slight smile and said, "I really do mean it. I don't like being the reason that Jesus died on the cross."

Uncle Samuel smiled and looked seriously into Theodore's eyes and said, "Well, son, we are all responsible for His crucifixion. I'm glad

The Dog Was Adopted Too

you really do understand about Jesus' cross and forgiveness."

Theodore sniffed and said, "Well, I need to ask your forgiveness for the way that I acted when I first came to live with you," said Theodore. "Until Alex told me that you said you wanted me before my parents died and had tried to make me happy, I didn't think that you loved me at all. I guess that's what kept me from giving you a chance."

"Thank you" said Uncle Samuel, "But there is nothing to be forgiven for. You were so hurt, sad, and confused when you moved in with us. We understood what was wrong with you but, we just didn't know how to reach you."

"I was so mixed up then. I guess I still am, sort of," admitted Theodore.

"Well, could you tell us what started this change in your thinking?" asked Aunt Betty.

"It might sound strange, but it was a dog, the one named Wally."

Aunt Betty said, "Wally! That's the dog that bit Alex, isn't it? How did he help you?"

"You see, when I came to live with you, I didn't know about the agreement that you had with my folks. I thought that you just had to take me in. Anyway, Frances was telling Alex and me that she loved Wally and that his owner had to find a new home for him. I liked the way that she loved Wally before she adopted him. I always wished that you had loved me before you adopted me."

He saw that his aunt and uncle were about to object, so he put his hand up and continued quickly. "Wait. Now, I know the truth, but first I thought that I was unwanted, and it made me feel sad all of the time."

"Theodore, we're sorry," stated Aunt Betty. "We honestly didn't know what to do. I'm glad that Wally and Alex helped you. It is wonderful having you smile. You don't know how happy our hearts are. We love you so much."

"Me too," Theodore said with a smile. "I'm okay about my adoption, but now I'd like to talk about my salvation again. Alex said that Jesus died for my sins and that He is waiting for me to ask Him to save me. Alex told me that I can't save myself, or if I could, it would have been silly for Jesus to die on the cross. I want to know more about Jesus. I want to be saved."

Aunt Betty and Uncle Samuel both jumped up from their chairs.

Theodore was surprised and jumped up too and found himself wrapped up in a group hug. He felt so happy.

Uncle Samuel said joyfully, "Let's pray, and then call Pastor Joe to see how soon he can see us." He prayed, "Thank you, Jesus, for giving Theodore to us. Amen."

Aunt Betty, with her head bowed said, "Thank you Jesus for healing our family. Thank you for touching Theodore's heart."

Theodore prayed, "God, I'm sorry for sinning. Please forgive me. Thank you for saving me from my sins. Amen."

It happened again. Theodore found himself being squeezed by the two happiest people he had ever seen. Uncle Samuel called Pastor Joe who said that he would meet them at the church in a half hour.

Before long, Mr. and Mrs. Bennett were thanking Pastor Joe for helping Theodore. The trip home was spent discussing what Pastor Joe had said.

Uncle Samuel parked the car, walked onto the porch, unlocked the door, and the three of them stepped inside.

Theodore said, "I feel so good. I feel like something has changed."

Uncle Samuel smiled and said loudly, "Praise God!" Once again there was a group hug.

Aunt Betty smiled and said, "Let's go to bed. We all have a big day tomorrow."

Theodore went to his bedroom but he wasn't sleepy. He thought over everything that he had learned. He sat at his desk and began to write what he wanted to share at the park tomorrow.

After a while his thoughts began to slow down. He finished writing and put his paper and pen away. He was so happy.

He began to get ready for bed. He took the envelope from the pocket of his robe and started to open it but thought better of it. He got up and found his aunt and uncle in the kitchen.

Aunt Betty said in surprise, "We thought you were asleep by now."

"I couldn't sleep," he said as he held the envelope out to his aunt. "I found this in the laundry room."

Opening the envelope, Aunt Betty smiled and said, "I had forgotten about this letter." Motioning with her hand she said, "Come sit at the table. Samuel, you come too."

She pulled a letter and a magazine clipping out and laid it on the table for all to see. She read, "Dear Sis, I found this picture in a magazine. I think Theodore will look so cute in it. You are so good at sewing. Can you help me find a pattern for it and give me pointers on how to make it? Yes, the baby will be born in a few weeks. If the baby is a girl we will name her Rhonda and if a boy we will name him Ronald. We have Theodore's old baby bed. Theodore is so sweet. He told us that his baby can have the bed because he is a 'big boy' now. We will see you in a few days. Love, Christine."

Theodore turned the magazine picture around and said, "Hey, I remember that suit. I wore it a lot until it got too small. Ronnie even wore it until he was too big for it."

Uncle Samuel looked at the picture and said, "Yes. I've seen that suit quite a few times."

"We worked on that suit for two days before it was complete," said Aunt Betty. "It was your Easter gift, and you were so proud wearing it to church. I'll look through our pictures and see if I have one with you wearing it."

Theodore smiled and said, "Thanks."

Aunt Betty leaned over, gave Theodore a hug and said, "You're welcome."

Uncle Samuel said, "That's a fine memory to go to bed with."

Hugs were exchanged and Theodore went to his room. He went to bed and soon drifted off to sleep. His dreams were like sweet visits with his parents and Ronnie.

Chapter Twenty
Sunday Morning
The Contest

The world seemed to be upside down in four households. Michael, Derick, and Joshua Davis, Theodore Moore, Kevin Oliver, and Alex Foster were all dressed at least a half-hour before their parents. Instead of, "Hurry up, Son!" the statements were more like, "Please hurry, Dad," or "Mom, I'll be disqualified if I'm late!"

Alex got into the van first and buckled his seat belt. He studied his contest entry while he waited for the rest of the family. Leora, and her friends piled into the rear seat and buckled up. Mom and Dad got in. The van began backing up and Leora shouted, "Buckle up!" Dad stopped the van and he and Mom put on their seat belts. Dad backed the van out of the driveway and headed for church.

The trips to the church were backwards, also. The parents were chatting about the special evening service at the park while the boys were silently reading their contest entries and trying to think of other items to add.

The cars of the four families drove into the church parking lot at almost the same moment. Doors flew open and the six excited, whooping boys ran across the parking lot. The glass entrance door was open and the noisy boys all squeezed through and ran down the hall toward their classroom. The room was quiet and empty except for Mr. Walker, who was sitting at his desk reading. He jumped when the six boys stampeded through the door and slapped their sheets of paper on his desk.

The Dog Was Adopted Too

He laughed as he took each paper and straightened out the wrinkles.

"Well, boys," he said, "the way that you're acting, I think this is going to be an exciting contest."

The boys surrounded Mr. Walker's desk and each one told him how hard he had studied. Within the next two minutes, the rest of the students had drifted in and Mr. Walker collected 2 more entries.

He asked everyone to be seated and said, "Mr. Jenkins isn't here, today, so I'll check your answers myself. Split into pairs and study your salvation memory verses while I read the entries."

The class spoke in low tones as Mr. Walker studied the answers. Eight minutes later, he announced, "I have the results and you aren't going to believe what I found."

The class instantly became quiet and focused on Mr. Walker. "One student found seven items; another found eight and four more of you found nine. The surprising thing is that the last two entries have produced a tie! Alex and Theodore each found eleven items."

The class as a unit whispered, "Eleven!"

Theodore asked, "Does that mean that we both win?"

Mr. Walker said, "Not necessarily." The classroom buzzed with questions and suggestions. Mr. Walker raised his hands and said, "Wait! I have a tiebreaker. Have you heard of a Spiritual truth?" The class was quiet. He said, "A Spiritual truth is like an example of how a Bible story can be applied to our lives today. Each truth will help us know God's will and how He wants us to live. There are several spiritual truths in this story. I'll give you a couple of examples.

"Peter climbed out of the boat so he could walk on the water to Jesus. The Spiritual truth is: You have to get out of your 'comfort zone' to do God's will. Peter's boat is like our comfort zone.

"Another Spiritual truth involves Peter when he took his eyes off of Jesus and sank into the water. The water is like sin. Keeping your eyes on Jesus will keep you from sinking into sin.

"Do you understand?" A sea of nodding heads told Mr. Walker that they did. "The first boy who finds one more Spiritual truth will be the winner. When the second hand reaches twelve, you have five minutes."

Alex and Theodore opened their Bibles to Matthew 14 and turned them face down on the table. Mr. Walker looked at the clock on the wall, which made all the boys turn to watch it. The second hand swept past the numbers and then it reached ten.

Everyone chanted, "10... 9... 8... 7... 6... 5... 4... 3... 2...1," and shouted, "Go!"

Both boys flipped their Bibles over and began reading. Theodore placed his finger on the page and traced each word from left to right all the way down the page. Alex leaned over his Bible and began reading the scriptures. The scar on his hand began stinging so he rubbed the spot while he read.

Mr. Walker warned, "Four minutes."

Alex continued to read. The movie screen in his mind began playing his dream about when he was Peter walking on the water. He remembered how excited he had felt about really being able to see Jesus. The cold wind had been pushing him; the stinging rain had pelted his skin and soaked his hair and clothes.

The class shouted, "Three!"

He had looked down at the water, had taken his eyes off of Jesus and had sunk into the waves.

The class of timekeepers loudly chimed, "Two!"

Alex felt his heart beating faster as he relived the drama of the dream. In his vivid imagination, he saw his hand reaching up toward Jesus through the pouring rain and over the sound of the wind he could hear himself shout, "Jesus, save me!"

Voices rattled the room, "One!"

Alex closed his eyes, trying to concentrate on the scene in his head. He continued to massage his hand and pressed on a sore spot just at the moment he saw Jesus reach down to Peter. Suddenly, the pictures in his mind froze. He focused on Jesus' hand and saw something he hadn't thought of before.

He jumped up from his chair and exclaimed, "I have one! When Peter shouted, 'Jesus save me,' Jesus grabbed him with perfect hands, because Jesus was only saving his life. But when I asked Jesus to 'save me from my sins,' Jesus had been crucified and saved me with nail scarred hands because he was saving my SOUL!"

Mr. Walker raised his arms, jumped up and shouted, "We have a winner!"

The class cheered, jumped to their feet, and gathered around Alex, congratulating him with slaps on his back and high-fives. Mr. Walker asked everyone to be seated and handed Alex his two hard-earned tickets.

Theodore walked over to Alex, patted him on his back, and said, "Congratulations." He went back to his seat and sat quietly.

Mr. Walker returned to his desk. He took in a deep breath and as he blew it out he said, "That was good!" He quieted the class and asked Alex, "How did you think of the Spiritual truth about the scars on Jesus' hands? I hadn't thought of that one."

Alex said, "You told us that the water that Jesus walked on can be thought of as sin. Well, Peter's life was saved before the crucifixion, so there wouldn't have been any scars on Jesus' hands. But when I asked Him to save me from my sins, it was after the crucifixion, so Jesus did have the nail scars in His hand."

Mr. Walker said, "That is wonderful reasoning. Whew! I've got to calm myself down if I'm going to teach this lesson. Okay, first, let's say the salvation memory verses that you have been studying."

Alex joined the class in reciting the verses but glanced at Theodore, who was staring out the window. He worried that he might be upset about losing the contest. He decided to talk to him after class.

After Mr. Walker's closing prayer, some of the boys followed Alex, hinting about being the one invited to go bowling. Alex said, "I'll let the lucky fellow know."

The boys divided into smaller groups and Alex hurried and caught up with Theodore. He slowed to a walk and asked, "Would you like to be my bowling guest?"

Theodore smiled, and said, "Sure."

Alex asked, "Are you okay?"

Theodore replied, "Yeah, I'm just thinking."

The two friends walked quietly to the worship service and each boy sat with his own family.

After the final hymn and the closing prayer, Pastor Joe said, "Remember 'Praise in the Park' which begins at 2 PM, followed by praise time."

Alex and his family filed down the aisle toward the door and shook Pastor Joe's hand as they left. Alex reached into his pocket and smiled as he felt the bowling passes.

Pastor Joe said, "Alex, you look pleased."

Alex pulled the passes from his pocket and said, "I won the Sunday school contest."

Pastor Joe said, "Well, congratulations."

Alex shook Pastor Joe's hand again, and said, "Thank you." He trotted outside, joined his family and showed them his passes.

"Who are you going to invite?" asked Leora.

"I've already invited Theodore," Alex answered.

"That was really nice," Mom said, "I bet he was happy about that."

"I think so," said Alex. He sat in the van and stared quietly out the window as his dad drove home. He wondered what Theodore might have been thinking about.

Chapter Twenty-One
Sunday Afternoon and Evening
Praise in the Park

Alex felt like he was in the military. After church and a quick lunch, his mom became a drill sergeant. His family arrived at the park at 1PM with a vanload of supplies, just minutes ahead of the pastor and a few other families. It seemed that each car had its own drill sergeant and before 2PM the park was decorated and ready for "Praise in the Park".

Families began arriving at 2:00 and by 2:30, the parking area was nearly full. Baseball, dodge ball, horseshoes, and a game of chase produced mixed sounds of laughter and cheers. People ate at tables in the pavilion, at open-air picnic tables, or sat on table cloths on the grass. Everywhere there was conversation and laughter.

As Sunday afternoon faded into evening, the food was put away. The people began to follow the string of lights that lined the path to the lake. Friends and families sitting in chairs or on the ground formed a ring around a campfire in the center of the common area. The pleasant aroma from the fire and the quiet hum of voices drifted throughout the park. Lights and camp fires from near-by campers blinked through the trees in the wooded area. The reflection of the moon gently danced on the lake.

Hymns were sung and joyful eyes sparkled in the firelight. Pastor Joe preached a brief sermon about Jesus being in a garden many times during His earthly ministry. After a closing hymn, the pastor said, "We came here tonight to share praises of what God has been doing in our lives. Theodore Moore would like to speak to you first." Theodore blushed as faces turned toward him, and for a moment, it seemed that he might change his mind. Pastor Joe motioned for him to stand next to him. Theodore picked up a sheet of paper and joined him near the fire.

Theodore looked at the group surrounding him. The light from the camp fire flickered on the faces of people who had become his new family and friends. His aunt and uncle were sitting directly in front of him beside Alex and his family. To his left sat Mr. Norton, Frances, Wally, and Mrs. Pam. To his right, on the other side of Alex, Mr. Walker sat with his family, which was next to Pastor Joe's family. Scattered throughout the ring of people he was able to pick out the faces of, Michael, Derick, Joshua, and Kevin.

Theodore's heart filled with happiness. He smiled as he looked down at his paper and tilted it slightly toward the camp fire.

Timidly, he began reading, "I want to tell you what happened to me." He looked up and said, "It all started months ago." He tried not to grin too big as he looked at his aunt and uncle who were smiling at him.

He looked around at the circle of happy faces and began again, "All of you probably know that my parents died and my brother was sent to live with another aunt and uncle. Because I didn't think that my aunt and uncle loved me, I was sad for a long time. Aunt Betty and Uncle Samuel tried everything to help me to become happy, but I didn't know how to stop being sad. I didn't have any friends here. I had been made to leave all of my friends when my parents died and I had to move. I didn't even want to go to church."

He pointed in the direction of Frances, Mr. Norton, and Wally. He said, "I met Frances in this park one day when she was walking her dog, Wally." When the dog heard his name, he happily wagged his tail. Theodore continued, "Frances and her dad became my friends and talked me into going to church, which made my family happy."

When Theodore said the word "family" his aunt and uncle beamed with pride.

"Wally is the reason that my life began to get better. When Frances told me how much she loved Wally and then was able to adopt him, it made me want to be loved by my adopted family."

Theodore pointed his paper toward Mr. Walker and said, "Mr.

The Dog Was Adopted Too

Walker always made me feel welcome in his Sunday school class, so when I started wanting friends I asked him to help me. He talked to Alex and after Wally got hit by the car, Alex and I started to become friends." Theodore looked back down at his paper, found his place and continued, "Soon Alex helped me to meet more of his friends, both at church and at school. With Alex's help, I found out that my aunt and uncle had always loved me. I was happier, but I still felt like I needed something else. That's when I started asking questions."

"I visited Frances and Mr. Norton a lot. They helped me to understand how God had helped them when Mrs. Norton had died."

Theodore looked up and smiled at Mrs. Pam and continued, "Mrs. Pam told me that when her husband died everything went wrong. She didn't have water, and a storm messed up her house. She was cold and got sick a lot. She felt alone until her friends helped her to see that God was always with her. Finally, she got a job, a car, and a house! She said that now when she has problems, she knows that God still helps her.

"I thought about what Mrs. Pam had said and the 'Broken Toy' story that Frances had told me. When Alex told me the 'Mud' story, I knew that I needed to be a Christian, but I didn't know how.

"Today's Sunday school contest was about Peter walking on the water. Alex and I were in a tie and needed one more answer to decide who would win. Alex answered first and won. He told us that when Peter asked Jesus to save him, Jesus had saved his life by pulling him up from the water with perfect hands. And then, Alex said that when he asked Jesus to save him, He did. Jesus didn't save him from water but from sin. Alex said that Jesus saved his soul by pulling him up from his sins, with nail scarred hands."

The people applauded and Theodore stopped reading and smiled at the crowd. Some people were congratulating Alex.

When everyone settled down again, Theodore continued. "After Sunday school, I thought about everything that I had been told this week and I put it all together like a jigsaw puzzle." He turned slightly to shine more light on his paper and read:

- "Mrs. Pam said that God loved her even when things went wrong.
- I learned from Frances' "Broken Toy Story" that I need to let God keep my problems so He can fix them.
- "The Mud Story" showed me that I need God's forgiveness for

my sins before I can go to heaven.

Theodore continued, "Last night when I talked to Uncle Samuel and Aunt Betty they took me to talk to Pastor Joe.

"Pastor Joe said that one reason that I'd been so sad was because I didn't know that my aunt and uncle had loved me all my life. And another reason I was sad was because I didn't know that God had loved me all my life, too. He said that just like I was adopted by Uncle Samuel and Aunt Betty and had become their son, God wanted to adopt me so I would be His son."

Theodore looked at Pastor Joe and asked, "How'd you say that?"

"You did fine," Pastor Joe answered. Then, to the listeners he said, "What Theodore is talking about is found in Romans 8:14-15. The Bible says that the Holy Spirit leads you to receive the spirit of adoption, and you can call God, 'Abba Father!' Abba means daddy. Now, how cool is that?

"Theodore, you didn't have to do anything to be adopted by your aunt and uncle. They did all of the work because they loved you and wanted you. Your new folks can't 'un-adopt' you either. That is how God is. You need to ask Jesus to come into your heart. Jesus did all of the work for you on the cross."

Pastor Joe looked back at the group and continued, "Last night I told Theodore about the word 'grace.' Grace is something that God gives to you as a gift. You can't earn grace. The Bible says in Ephesians 2:8; 'For by grace are ye saved through faith; and that not of yourselves: it is the gift of God.'"

He looked at the people and added, "Theodore was also worried about being sad. I told him that right now he was happier because he has new friends, which is good, but none of his friends can bring him the kind of joy that God gives. In Philippians 4:6 Jesus tells us not to worry, but to be thankful and tell God our problems. The next verse, Philippians 4:7, says, 'And the peace of God, which passeth all understanding, shall keep your hearts and minds through Christ Jesus.' That's where our joy will always come from." Pastor Joe smiled at Theodore and nodded.

Theodore responded with a smile. He took a deep breath, and began to speak. Suddenly a log slipped in the fire. Sparks jumped up and sizzling and crackling could be heard as new wood caught on fire. Theodore jumped back, the people gasped and some of them jumped

The Dog Was Adopted Too

to their feet. Wally jumped up and barked. Frances grabbed the startled dog and settled him down. The mass of people laughed at themselves.

Pastor Joe said, "Now that God has gotten your attention, continue Theodore."

After the laughter quieted, the people sat down and Theodore began again. "Pastor Joe helped me a lot. I was so worried about being sad that I didn't see that I already had a family who loved me. I felt so good when I got home after talking to him.

Theodore looked up from his paper and said, "Then I learned more today in Sunday school:

- Today's contest about Peter walking on the water taught me to stay focused on Jesus.
- And when Alex explained about Jesus' nail-scarred hands, I was sure that Jesus really did die on the cross to save me."

After church I talked to Pastor Joe, again. He told me that when I pray for my salvation, and ask Jesus to forgive me and become my Savior, I will be adopted by God, and He will be my heavenly daddy. He will never stop loving me or give up on me."

Theodore reached up and through cupped hands, whispered in Pastor Joe's ear. He whispered back into Theodore's ear. Theodore turned and facing the smiling faces said, "In John 10:29, the Bible says...Uh." Uncertainly he looked up at Pastor Joe and back down at his paper. He smiled, looked up and continued. "The Bible says that nobody can take me out of God's hands." He looked up at Pastor Joe who smiled and nodded. Smiling brightly he announced, "Right then I knew that I was ready. I prayed and asked Jesus to forgive me of my sins and to be my Savior. Now I'm a Christian, and I've been adopted again! And not only that, soon I'll be baptized."

Cheers and whistles echoed across the park. People jumped up and for several minutes Theodore shook hands and received hugs. He could feel his heart pounding with happiness.

Everyone returned to their places and Theodore started to sit down, too. Some of the people began asking him to tell the "The Broken Toy Story" and "The Mud Story". Pastor Joe called Theodore back by his side and with an encouraging smile nudged his arm.

Theodore looked around at all of his new friends and, with a happy smile he began telling "The Broken Toy Story". He began, "A little girl went to a repairman so he could fix her broken doll. She gave the doll to the man, but before he could fix it, she grabbed it back and cried as she hugged it. The repairman said, 'I can't fix it if you don't let me hold it.'"

Looking at Theodore, Alex whispered to his dad, "I'm glad that Theodore is my friend."

Mr. Foster said, "I believe that God used you to help him to get saved."

"Yeah," Alex said. "I believe that Jesus used him to show me that I had only been worrying about myself and ignoring the people around me." Alex looked up at his dad and said, "You were right. I was self-centered."

"Are you 'Jesus centered', now?" Mr. Foster asked.

Alex beamed, "Yes sir. Well, I'm sure trying to be."

Mr. Foster smiled proudly and put his arm around his son as they continued to listen to Theodore's stories.

Alex looked at the people around the campfire. He could see the pleasure in their faces as they listened to Theodore. He thanked God for such wonderful times as this. He thought that the disciples must have listened to Jesus by the light of a campfire, just like this. He sighed happily and thought, "This is going to be another happy memory."

Alex listened to the sound of Theodore's voice and the crackle of the campfire. Another log slipped, sending a shower of sparks toward the sky. Alex watched as the miniature fires raced toward the moon. The clouds reflected the moonlight and off in the distance Alex could hear a duck laughing at a duck joke.

God smiled.

"CREDITS

"The Broken Toy Story" and "The Mud Story" were affectionately drawn from memories of pulpit stories at church when I was young, over 50 years ago. Original authorship is unknnown.

THE DOG WAS ADOPTED TOO

www.ingramcontent.com/pod-product-compliance
Lightning Source LLC
Chambersburg PA
CBHW050540300426
44113CB00012B/2196